GET YOUR BEST PEOPLE
TO GIVE THEIR BEST EFFORT

Your Go-To Guide for Recognizing and Defeating
Impostor Syndrome in Your Bold and Brilliant Teams

MAUREEN ZAPPALA

Copyright © 2025 by High Altitude Strategies
All rights reserved. No part of this publication may be reproduced, distributed or transmitted in any form or by any means, including photocopying, recording, or other electronic or mechanical methods, without the prior written permission of the publisher, except in the case of brief quotations embodied in critical reviews and certain other noncommercial uses permitted by copyright law. For permission requests, write to the publisher, addressed "Attention: Permissions Coordinator," at the address below.
Edited by Hope Bollinger Soto
Cover design: Gina Zappala
Publisher's Cataloging-in-Publication Data

Names: Zappala, Maureen, author.
Title: Get your best people to give their best effort : your go-to guide for recognizing and defeating impostor syndrome in your bold and brilliant team / by Maureen Zappala.
Description: Henderson, NV: High Altitude Strategies, 2024.
Identifiers: LCCN: 2024918782 | ISBN: 979-8-9910966-0-7 (hardcover) | 979-8-9910966-1-4 (paperback) | 979-8-9910966-2-1 (audio) | 979-8-9910966-3-8 (ebook)
Subjects: LCSH Leadership. | Success in business. | Success--Psychological aspects. | Impostor phenomenon. | Employees--Coaching of. | Psychology, Industrial. | Self-actualization (Psychology) | BISAC BUSINESS & ECONOMICS / Leadership | BUSINESS & ECONOMICS / Careers / Career Advancement & Professional Development | BUSINESS & ECONOMICS / Management | BUSINESS & ECONOMICS / Mentoring & Coaching | BUSINESS & ECONOMICS / Workplace Culture
Classification: LCC HD38.2 .Z37 2024 | DDC 658--dc23

High Altitude Strategies
Henderson, Nevada
Printed in the United States of America

To every boss I've ever had, including my quirky supervisor, Dick Witter, at my very first part-time summer job when I was 16, my kind summer internship boss at Wright Patterson AFB, Harry Snowball, my fantastic NASA chief, John Schaefer, and my amazing Las Vegas La-Z-Boy store manager, Debbie Reighard.

To all the role models, mentors and teachers I've had. especially my 5th grade math teacher, Sister Consilio, at St. Charles School on Staten Island. She took extra time after school to teach me long division because I was out sick on the day she covered it in class. She simply said, "Wow. You picked that up quickly." That launched me to love math, which came in handy during my brutal Differential Equations class in college.

I learned about great leadership, not because I was a great leader, but because I was led, inspired and encouraged by extraordinary ones.

Table of Contents

Introduction 7
1. Is it Possible? 21
2. Impostor Syndrome History 25
3. Jan's Journey 33
4. You Mean I'm Normal? 37
5. Locked Down and Shaken Up 43
6. Men vs. Women? 51
7. The Impostor Test 55
8. Be Like Mel Gibson 59
9. Impostor Syndrome and Intelligence Theories 67
10. Understand the Effect. Then Expect. 79
11. Response to Success and Failure 85
12. Is This a "Woo-woo" Topic? 91
13. The Dreaded Skill Gap 95
14. Impostor Syndrome Is NOT a Superpower 101
15. Jan's Journey: After 105
16. When the CEO is the CEI 111
17. Feeding the Insecurity Monster 117
18. Make Friends Who Make Memories 125
19. Set Up for Failure? 129
20. Let Them Fail 133
21. Fueled Up! 141
22. Character Matters 147
23. Flip the Scripts 153
24. Teach Someone Something 157
25. Don't Fake it Till You Make It 161
    Appendix A: Character Trait Assessment 167
    Appendix B: Coaching Strategies 171
    Appendix C: Journal Prompts 175
    About the Author 179
    Acknowledgements 181

Introduction

Unmasking the Superstars

Would it surprise you to know that some of your top performers feel incompetent? Or that many of your most accomplished team members feel like they're one mistake away from being exposed as a fraud? Ouch. You're probably guiding a talented, high-achieving team that delivers exceptional results. On the surface, they're brimming with confidence, but behind this polished exterior, many wrestle with the nagging self-doubt known as impostor syndrome.

Impostor syndrome is the persistent belief held by competent people where they think they are not as qualified as others think they are. They attribute their successes to luck or timing, and fear being exposed as frauds. This leads to overwork, procrastination, and perfectionism, while also preventing them from celebrating achievements and growing in their careers. Leaders may not readily spot and address impostor syndrome in others because it hides behind high performance. Team members might look like they're thriving, yet feel unqualified and undeserving of success. Their internal struggles can lead to burnout, reduced job satisfaction, and a dip in overall productivity.

As a professional keynote speaker, I've presented on the topic of impostor syndrome for close to fifteen years. I've addressed thousands of people, for dozens of clients across a variety of industries. My audiences include all levels. Blue-collar, white-collar, new employees, C-Suite, middle managers, technical, administrative, creatives…every demographic you can imagine. Everywhere I go, I meet people who struggle with the tension of how their internal emotions don't match the external data that says they're qualified and competent.

Impostor syndrome isn't rare. The often-quoted statistic is that 70 percent of professionals will experience it at some point. I think the actual number is much higher, but it's like trying to trace a shadow that shifts. Some data show 90 percent, some show 60 percent. Much of the data is so narrowed, like "impostor syndrome among Hispanic HR professional in construction in the UK." How can you extrapolate that to the general population?

It's a personal and intimate experience for many, especially leaders. I once keynoted an event with an audience of close to 800 people. When I finished, I chatted with audience member and I noticed a distinguished gentleman off to the side, patiently waiting to talk to me. When I was free, he came over, and led me to a quiet part of the convention ballroom. He said quietly, "Thank you for this! I've got impostor syndrome, and this was what I needed!" The man was the organization's CEO.

While my strategies are effective for individuals, I've observed that leaders often lack the tools to support their teams struggling with impostor syndrome. Regardless of whether you experience it, as a leader, you must understand and address it in your team members. The dirty little secret is this: The single most significant obstacle preventing your team from reaching their greatest potential is not a lack of training, resources, or confidence—it's impostor syndrome. This book breaks from the pack by focusing on this hidden issue, providing tools to recognize and strategies to conquer it.

You, as a leader, may or may not experience impostor syndrome. That's not the issue. The issue is that you have team members who do, and you are responsible to lead, develop, and inspire them. Understanding impostor syndrome will make you a better leader.

Introduction

Browse any bookstore, and you'll find oodles of leadership books covering a huge array topics from enhancing emotional intelligence, developing strategic thinking, and making effective decisions. Be a unicorn leader, a data-driven leader, a servant leader, a leader who starts with why. Find the leadership road map, the 21 steps, the levels, the habits, the code, the superpowers. There's advice on how to motivate, mediate, delegate, navigate, negotiate, celebrate, educate, resonate, appreciate, collaborate, coordinate, de-escalate, humiliate (don't read that book), infuriate (or that one), and strategiate (I made that word up.) Want to provide feedback? It's covered. Want to foster a thriving company culture? Ditto. Want a leader to model yourself after? You can lead like Lasso, Lincoln, Jesus, a woman, a marine or a pirate.

Despite this wealth of knowledge, the one crucial subject that is either overlooked or under-emphasized is impostor syndrome. This hidden issue can quietly eat away at even the most capable individuals, yet it rarely takes center stage in leadership discussions. This book isn't just another leadership guide—it's a crucial resource for uncovering and nurturing the true potential of your best people, who might be held back by their own silent doubts. If you really want to get your best people to give their best effort, this is the best place to start.

This is not just an individual issue, but an organizational one. Leaders play a key role in creating an environment where team members feel valued and confident. By becoming more aware of it, you can help your team members unmask their true potential. This book will guide you in this mission, turning impostor syndrome from a hidden saboteur into a catalyst for growth and empowerment.

What's first?

Stephen Covey said, "Seek first to understand, then to be understood." Similarly, St. Francis of Assisi emphasized understanding over being understood. Haruki Murakami noted,

Get Your Best People to Give Their Best Effort

"Just because you understand it doesn't mean you can explain it." I relate to this struggle.

I have extensive content on impostor syndrome: my keynotes, video series, a book, blogs, emails, and hours of research. It's a challenge for me to be concise in describing it. I needed some litmus test to help determine which content stays and which content goes. What does the leader really need the most? They've told me they want to learn how to lead people through impostor syndrome. But what about the leaders who don't even know their people have it? If their most significant focus is to get their best people to give their best effort, how can I guide them to do that?

Suddenly it was clear.

Understand first, lead second. Leaders must grasp impostor syndrome before guiding their teams through it. This book follows a two-part structure: understanding impostor syndrome and leading through it.

Understanding impostor syndrome fosters empathy, trust, and opens communication. It leads to better goal-setting, achievements, celebrations, constructive feedback, mentoring, and training. You'll see increased productivity, more creativity, and better decision-making in your team. Your leadership effectiveness will grow as you model resilience and self-compassion, reducing burnout and turnover. The journey may be messy, but the destination is pretty cool.

By understanding first and leading second, you'll get your best people to give their best effort and be the best boss they've ever had. So, let's go. Understand first. Lead second.

Who am I?

I was born in Glen Cove, a Long Island suburb of New York City. I'm the baby, with an older sister and brother, and a twin brother...older than me by four minutes. We moved to Staten Island when I was about five. My dad was an engineering technician for the Port Authority of New York and New Jersey (originally called the Port of New York Authority.) He was not a college graduate, but he managed to work his way up the

Introduction

organization, starting out as a Port Authority cop in the Holland Tunnel. I adored my dad. In 1969, when I was almost eight years old, I was with him in the driveway of our Staten Island home hovering over the engine of our family car—a Ford Country Squire "woodie" station wagon. Dad was doing what he loved the most, tinkering with cars. I was doing what I loved the most, hanging with Dad.

I was curious about how the engine worked. So I pummeled him with questions. "Daddy, what's that for? What's that do? How does this work?" Finally, he looked at me and said "Maureen, when you grow up, you should be an engineer."

I was appalled. "Yuk! No, Daddy! I don't want to drive a train!"

He laughed. "No, Maureen, not that kind of engineer! I mean the kind who designs and fixes things, like machines. Or buildings, bridges and tunnels." Growing up in NYC, surrounded by buildings, bridges and tunnels, I loved the idea, and my dream was born.

A few years later, he came home from work one evening with a big roll of paper which he called, "blueprints." He unfurled them onto the dining room table, and I was mesmerized. I didn't know what I was looking at, but it was the prettiest thing I'd ever seen. I scanned the images with the beautiful lines and arrows and symbols, almost holding my breath. Then I read the words in the lower right-hand corner: World Trade Center.

"What's that, Daddy?" I asked.

He replied, with enormous gusto and pride, "It's going to be two buildings! Twins! Just like you!"

My dad's role in the project centered on the developing the massive Port Authority Trans-Hudson (PATH) transportation hub underneath the Twin Towers. Growing up in the shadow of the World Trade Center was a joy. Watching the construction project was entertainment. When the buildings were complete, my dad took an office on the seventy-something floor, with a spectacular view of Manhattan. It was always a treat to visit him in his office, and eat at the executive cafeteria, a stunning modern

Get Your Best People to Give Their Best Effort

facility decked out in red, white, blue, and chrome. I loved the Twin Towers, and I was proud of my dad.

Sadly, he passed away while I was in high school, and he never got to see me continue my education and head off to college. But the dream of becoming an engineer never left me.

In 1978, during my high school senior year, I applied to my top college choice, University of Notre Dame. I had good grades, and an outstanding SAT score. But I was wait-listed! What? Why? I didn't know it at the time, but Notre Dame had only been coed for about 7–8 years, and they were short on women's dorms, so it was really competitive for women to get admitted. I jumped into action and asked a boatload of people to write letters of recommendation for me. Past teachers, family friends, my dad's colleagues, my former bosses, my parish priest... anyone and everyone. Then I waited.

I graduated high school on Sunday, May 20, 1979, and I still didn't know where I'd be going to college. The very next day, Monday, I received a fat envelope from Notre Dame. Acceptance! Phew! Thank you, God!

I started in Civil Engineering, but in sophomore year, when I saw the curriculum included unappetizing (to me) classes like "Concrete" and "Wastewater Systems." I switched to Mechanical Engineering, and I loved it. I secured two summer internships at the Wright Patterson Air Force Base in Dayton Ohio, and fell in love with military aircraft engines. My concentration found me. But my confidence did not.

At Notre Dame, women made up only 22 percent of the student body. In engineering, the ratio was even smaller, closer to 10 percent. I was one of a tiny handful of women in the overwhelmingly male-dominated engineering world. I never got hung up on that, but sometimes it was very obvious. I remember being assigned to work on a team for our senior design project. Our group included four guys and me. I didn't know them very well, I was really shy and awkward and it was awful. By then, I had two summers of experience working with the Air Force where I was involved in some very cool cutting-edge technology. But in this group of men, I felt unseen and unheard. Part of it

Introduction

was on me. I was intimidated that they would not listen to my ideas or ask my opinion. I am not a forceful or loud person, but I felt like I had to be in order to be heard and contribute my ideas to the group.

It was the first time I'd ever experienced an overwhelming feeling of, "What the heck am I doing here? I don't belong, and I'm a fraud!"

In 1983, I graduated college with a bachelor's degree in mechanical engineering. The engineering job market was lousy. I wanted to work with jet engines, but there weren't many opportunities. Fortunately, I got an offer from the NASA Lewis Research Center in Cleveland, and I was elated. A job! With a fabulous paycheck! Working with jet engines! I didn't care that I knew nobody in Cleveland, or that it even was Cleveland. (The city had a terrible reputation in the '70s and '80s. Google "Cuyahoga burning river.") I was out of my mind excited to start work.

As my July 1983 start date approached, I was gripped with panic. I thought, *"This is NASA!* Where all the smart people are! The real rocket scientists! I won't fit in! Did NASA realize I'm not a straight-A student? What were they thinking when they hired me?"

By 1983, NASA-Lewis had not hired new engineers for almost fifteen years. They needed to build their workforce, so I was hired in a big pool of about 200 other engineers. We were called "the Fresh Outs" because we were hired fresh out of college. And just like college, it was overwhelmingly male-dominated, with a handful of women. It was a blast to have an instant circle of friends to do things with. But I soon realized the truth about why NASA hired me. They needed women.

It was true. NASA's goal was to make the agency "look like America" and they needed more minorities. I thought, *"So, that's why they hired me!"* I felt like the token female, somewhat used and a bit dismissed. Not fun. But the reality was that I was a perfect fit at NASA. My childhood dream, my good grades, my Air Force experience…it made sense that NASA hired me. Yes, they needed women, but I bubbled to the top of the list. It's just that

Get Your Best People to Give Their Best Effort

back then, I didn't really believe it. I felt I got the job by sheer luck.

In my first few months at NASA I was responsible for creating an analog computer model (Oh my! Isn't that yester-tech???!) to explore a potentially dangerous jet engine phenomenon called "engine stall." Despite a four-year degree, and two summers with Wright Patterson Air Force Base, I felt I was in over my head. I didn't know the computer system, or the complexities of engine stall, or what direction to go. Even with expert guidance from my supervisor and coworkers, I felt ignorant and unqualified. I was terrified to ask questions, fearing it would unmask my stupidity. I dreaded the weekly progress check-ins because I thought my coworkers were smarter than I was, and were making way more progress than I was.

But you couldn't tell from the outside. Every day, I arrived at work, dressed to the nines, smiling, happy, ready to work. I worked my tail off. Coming in early, working late. Every day I plugged along with my project, trying my hardest to get a grip on this overwhelming assignment. Every day I struggled with the constant internal voice that was screaming "You have no idea what you are doing, Maureen!" I was constantly in fear of being "found out." But I hid it well behind an agreeable disposition, dogged determination and a beautiful wardrobe.

It was exhausting. You would have thought I was confident, but I knew I was not. You saw something completely different from what I was feeling, and that made me feel even more disingenuous, which led to more guilt and shame.

After six months, I finally had the courage to tell my boss I wasn't enjoying the job. He was supportive (and I think he realized I was not producing anything of value), and we arranged a lateral transfer for me to the testing team of the Propulsion Systems Laboratory (PSL) the jet engine test facility. I was excited because it wasn't a desk job, but a test facility job, which meant hands-on work with real jet engines. My dream job!

I remember that first day in PSL. I was so excited to be there, but I was also intimidated because I had no testing experience. My first assignment in PSL was simple: observe the crew

Introduction

conducting an engine test. How hard is that? Show up. Shut up. Don't screw up.

I walked into the control room and was starstruck. It was all kinds of techie-beautiful. The walls were covered with monitors, dials and blinking lights. Counters with keyboards and clipboards, people on headsets, focused on their work. The mood was intense. There were about eighteen people in the room, all way more experienced than I was. Oh, and I was the only woman. No pressure.

I found one empty chair in the far corner, sat, and began to do my job. Observe.

But then I got the hiccups! I was humiliated. Eighteen heads snapped in my direction. It was as if I could hear every person think, "Who is SHE????? Who let HER in? She doesn't belong here."

I know everyone gets hiccups. That's not the point. That story is not about hiccups. But hiccups tell the story that so many of us tell ourselves. Despite being qualified, competent and successful, so many of us feel like we're a hiccup away from others pointing their finger at us and saying, "You don't belong here, you fake, you fraud and phony."

That's impostor syndrome. It's the chronic fear of being found a fraud. It's the inability to internalize your success despite massive evidence of that success. It leaves a person feeling that they're not as smart as everyone thinks they are.

In this book, I'll share some of my story because in spite of a rocky start at NASA, I had a great career. I stayed in PSL, developed expertise in jet engine testing, published research, chaired conferences, was known around the world. I even was promoted to the Facility Manager of the PSL complex. Yet, there were so many moments I allowed my fraud fears to rob me of courage. I lived in a quiet fear for a long time. I thought something was wrong with me. It was years later I learned about impostor syndrome, and I felt a huge burden lift from me. I dove into the topic, researched and studied all I could. And as a result of my research, my experience and my reflections, you benefit. Because this book can help you not only work through your own

Get Your Best People to Give Their Best Effort

impostor syndrome, but it will help you lead your team through theirs.

I had great bosses at NASA. Carl Lorenzo, Ross Willoh, Frank Kutina, John Dicus, Wayne Thomas, Bruce Block, John Schaefer, Neil Saunders. They were all seriously good mentors, role models and friends. Yet, I not only wish I knew about impostor syndrome back then, I wish they did. I can only imagine how much more successful, influential and peaceful I (and everyone in our division!) would have been. Regardless, I'm glad I know now what I didn't know then. Now it's your turn.

Why This Book?

Today, as a professional speaker, and a lover of fashion, I appear to have it all together. But I still sometimes grapple with impostor syndrome, just like many of the individuals you lead. You wouldn't know it by looking at me, which is precisely the problem. *Leaders often don't realize the extent to which their team members are struggling.*

Many are reluctant to admit the struggle. The stigma associated with feeling like an impostor prevents people from seeking help. Even books with "impostor syndrome" in the title often go unread. As my business coach wisely said, those books don't pass the "First Class Test"—that is, would the people who fly first class feel comfortable displaying such a title in first class, surrounded by successful, wealthy experts? The implication is clear: admitting to impostor syndrome feels like admitting to a weakness that contradicts the image of success.

But as a leader, you want your best people to deliver their best effort. And to achieve this, it's your responsibility to remove the barriers to their brilliance. By recognizing and addressing impostor syndrome, you are equipping yourself with the tools to support your team in overcoming self-doubt, thus fostering a more confident and productive work environment.

Impostor syndrome also has organizational impact, making it a leadership challenge. By becoming informed about this pervasive issue, you are taking a proactive step toward stronger,

Introduction

more empathetic leadership. This, in turn, will empower your team to push past their self-imposed limitations, allowing their true potential to shine so that you can build more robust teams than make up amazing organizations. The bottom line is clear: *effective leadership involves not just managing tasks and outcomes, but also understanding and addressing the psychological and systemic barriers that hold your team back.* The result is a culture where everyone feels valued, capable, and ready to contribute their best efforts.

I'm not a leadership expert—I'm an impostor syndrome expert. But I've been led by extraordinary leaders who helped me on my anti-impostor journey. This book draws on those experiences, along with the content from my first book, *Pushing Your Envelope*, to equip you with tools to support your team. This book leans more on impostor syndrome than on leadership strategies. Leadership strategy resources are everywhere, but for insights into leading *through* impostor syndrome, this is your go-to guide, and I'm here to help.

Awkward interruption

It feels awkward to mention this, but there's a bit of an elephant in the room that I'd like to address. It may seem minor, but it's been brought to my attention enough that I thought I'd clarify it early in this book

There are two spellings of the word describing someone who fakes their identity. "Impostor" and "imposter;" both do the job, but here's a little backstory on why we've got two options.

"Impostor" is the older version, from the Latin word "impostorum"," which means to pose upon or deceive. This spelling has been the go-to in most English-speaking places and sticks to the pattern of other Latin-derived words like "actor" or "creator."

Then there's "imposter" with an 'er,' which popped up a bit later. It's an example of how English evolves, adapting spellings to fit how words sound. Today, it's pretty common and you'll see it used a lot in less formal settings.

Get Your Best People to Give Their Best Effort

Both "impostor" and "imposter" are accepted in dictionaries like Merriam-Webster and the Oxford English Dictionary. Historically, "impostor" was the norm in serious formal writing, but today, both versions are perfectly fine.

I've chosen to stick with the "or" spelling because so much of the impostor syndrome research comes from psychology and medicine, which historically uses the "or" version. The problem is that because most the more common spelling is with "er", I've occasionally been called out for "wrong spelling." But it's not wrong. It's simply less common.

PART ONE: UNDERSTAND FIRST

"Nothing in life is to be feared, it is only to be understood. Now is the time to understand more, so that we may fear less."

— *Marie Curie*

1

Is it Possible?

Dream for a minute.

You're the leader. Imagine walking into your office, where you're surrounded by team members who are confident and enthusiastic. They approach their work with boldness and creativity. Meetings are filled with innovative ideas, lively discussions, and a collective drive to excel. The hallway and cafeteria camaraderie is fun and friendly. In this environment, every individual feels valued and assured of their place, contributing their unique strengths.

Visualize a project kickoff where each team member readily volunteers for challenging roles, eager to stretch their capabilities and embrace new learning opportunities. There's no fear of judgment or failure, because the culture of your team is built on mutual support and recognition. Obstacles may arise, but team members are resilient, viewing setbacks as opportunities for growth rather than proof of incompetence. Self-doubt is replaced with self-assurance and constructive self-talk. Celebrations of success, both big and small, are frequent, and everyone's achievements are acknowledged, fostering a sense of shared accomplishment and pride.

Get Your Best People to Give Their Best Effort

This ripples through the organization. Productivity soars as team members are more focused and engaged, free from the mental burden of self-doubt. Collaboration reaches new heights as trust and open communication become the norm.

In this scenario, leadership is not micromanaging, constant cheerleading or hollow reassurance. Instead, it's guiding a team through addressing and overcoming impostor syndrome to unlock the full spectrum of their capabilities. It paves the way for a robust, innovative, agile and profitable organization where everyone can contribute their best, free from the hidden chains of self-doubt.

Yes, it is possible.

The Tangible Benefits

But there's more to the story. As impostor syndrome fades, so do its costly side effects. Mental health issues like anxiety and depression decrease, leading to fewer sick days. Presenteeism (when they show up to work even when they're sick, and underperform because they're sick) and quiet-quitting stop. With a healthier, more present team, productivity and efficiency are boosted, which helps lower operational costs.

Profits rise because the team's boosted creativity and problem-solving skills lead to innovative products and services, capturing more of the market. Customer satisfaction improves as a confident and engaged team delivers top-notch service. Plus, employee turnover drops, saving on recruitment and training expenses. The dreaded skill gap? It vanishes because capable employees believe they're ready for new challenges—and they succeed.

The workplace culture transforms, attracting high-potential talent wanting to join a supportive and energized environment. This influx of skilled professionals pushes the organization even further ahead, solidifying its position as an industry leader. The combined effect of higher productivity, lower costs, and increased innovation drives sustained financial growth and a strong competitive edge in the market.

Is it Possible?

By creating an environment that addresses and reduces impostor syndrome, you not only improve individual well-being, but also boost the organization's overall performance and profitability. Your leadership pays off in ways that go beyond the balance sheet, building a thriving, resilient, and dynamic workplace.

When you address the problem of impostor syndrome, everything changes.

This is exciting. Your role in solving the "I'm not good enough" poison cannot be overstated. As a leader, you have not only the responsibility but the authority to mitigate this. You also have the obligation. And now you'll have the tools. But where do you start?

Repeat: Understand First.

Seek to understand more about it first. You cannot battle an enemy unless you recognize the enemy. Make it your first priority to understand what impostor syndrome is, what it isn't, where it comes from, who it will affect, what is the effect, and what can you expect when your team in on the other side of it. Observe what your team members are doing so you can translate it to what they most likely are thinking. Impostor syndrome is a thought process distortion, so the more you can do to understand the distortion and undistort it, the better.

Your job is not to cheer them on with the "I believe in you" chant. If eliminating impostor syndrome was that easy, it would be…well…eliminated. But it's not. It takes work, especially by leaders who have team members inflicted with it. The temptation may be to quit trying to help, or think your team is stuck in the self-doubt, or that it's their issue to figure out. It may be tempting to believe the bad commentaries that say, "Impostor Syndrome is your Superpower! Embrace it." That piles on guilt and shame. You may even shy away from admitting you're familiar with it because you don't know how your team would respond.

Understand it anyway. Because once you can recognize not just the presence of impostor syndrome in your team, but the

Get Your Best People to Give Their Best Effort

detrimental and costly effect it is having on your organization, you'll be more driven and more committed to finding a way through its fog.

2

Impostor Syndrome History

The Impostor Syndrome, originally termed "Impostor Phenomenon," has a rich history dating back to 1978 when it was first identified by clinical psychologists Drs. Pauline Clance and Suzanne Imes in Atlanta, Georgia. Their groundbreaking paper, "The Impostor Phenomenon in High-Achieving Women: Dynamics and Therapeutic Interventions," emerged from their observations of chronic self-doubt among high-achieving female clients who, despite their success, often felt like frauds. A mere eight pages long, the paper laid the foundation for understanding the psychological roots and clinical implications of impostor feelings, focusing on high-achieving women. It provided a scientific framework for characterizing and recognizing the prevalence of what would later be commonly known as impostor syndrome.

Following the initial publication, interest in the topic grew. Clance's 1985 book, *The Impostor Syndrome: Overcoming the Fear that Haunts Your Success*, expanded on the original research, offering in-depth case studies and practical strategies for overcoming impostor feelings. Subsequent research revealed that impostor syndrome affects both men and women, though they may experience it differently. This finding broadened the scope of study beyond the initial focus on women. The phenomenon gained attention in various fields, including neuroscience, psychology, medicine, biochemistry, and sociology, leading to a growing body of research and literature. (If you can find Clance's book, get it! It reads like a novel. It's a brilliant and deeply satisfying book that feels very therapeutic and optimistic.)

Several key figures have contributed to the understanding and popularization of impostor syndrome. Valerie Young, co-founder (with Carolyn Herfurth) of the Impostor Syndrome Institute, published *The Secret Thoughts of Successful Women* in 2011. Despite its title, the book addresses impostor syndrome in both genders and offers practical advice for overcoming it in professional settings. High-profile individuals like Sheryl Sandberg, former Facebook COO, and Joyce Rochè, former Avon executive, have shared their personal experiences with impostor syndrome, bringing the concept into mainstream discourse. Amy Cuddy's 2012 TED Talk on body language further popularized the concept, discussing how both men and women experience impostor feelings.

Today, impostor syndrome is regarded as a common experience among high-achievers across genders and fields. It's not a medically catalogued psychiatric disorder included in the Diagnostic and Statistical Manual of Mental Disorders (DSM), but rather a persistent pattern of self-doubt and insecurity. Acknowledging these feelings is considered the first step in overcoming them. Recent approaches, like Young's work, emphasize addressing both individual experiences and external factors that contribute to impostor feelings.

As our understanding of impostor syndrome has evolved, so have the strategies for addressing it. What began as a clinical observation has grown into a widely recognized phenomenon that touches the lives of countless high-achievers. From its roots in psychology to its current place in popular culture, impostor syndrome research has shed light on the complex interplay between success, self-perception, and societal expectations. As we continue to explore this topic, we gain valuable insights into human psychology and the challenges faced by high-achievers in various fields, paving the way for more effective support and interventions for those grappling with feelings of being an impostor.

Recognizing and acknowledging these feelings is the first step to overcoming them. As Dr. Phil McGraw says, "You can't change what you don't acknowledge."

Defining Impostor Syndrome

So, what is impostor syndrome? Let's start with what it's not.

It's not a lack of self-esteem. Valerie Young says, "Self-esteem is a global sense we have about ourselves, where impostor syndrome is specific to our professional achievements in our education work and career arenas."

It's not a lack of education or resources or training or opportunity. People who struggle with impostor syndrome are often in organizations overflowing with these.

It's not simple humility or modesty where a person acknowledges their own true limits. That's actually a healthy response to self-doubt as we'll see later in this book.

It's not false modesty where a person pretends to be humble or self-deprecating, but is actually seeking affirmation and validation.

It's not a lack of confidence. People with impostor syndrome are usually the ones that are educated, elevated, celebrated. They're seen as competent and qualified, with some track record of success. Getting to that place requires quite a bit of confidence. They took the class, got the degree, applied for the job, had the interview, took on the role, assumed the responsibility. All of those took a measure of confidence.

It's not occasional self-doubt. It's normal to doubt one's own competence when faced with something new.

It's not the same as working hard, or seeking excellence or procrastinating. Those behaviors often accompany impostor syndrome, but by themselves, they're not a guarantee of experiencing it.

It's not being miserable in your chosen career. If you truly hate your job, it isn't a sign you have impostor syndrome. You may be in the wrong job for your skill set or your life's vision, or you felt pressured to go into a certain field. Or you may dislike certain elements of your job, like specific tasks or a certain co-worker. Being in the wrong job for you doesn't make you a fraud.

It's not true criminal fraudulence where you are intentionally deceiving people into believing you are something you are not. True frauds are people like Elizabeth Holmes, the founder and CEO the health technology company, Theranos, who was found guilty on four counts of defrauding investors. She claimed to have developed a revolutionary blood-testing device that required only a small amount of blood. It was later revealed that the technology did not work as promised and that the company had falsified test results and misled investors and patients. Or Frank Abagnale Jr. whose Wikipedia page describes a narrative of deception and fraud so absurd that it resembles a novel. He impersonated an airline pilot, a doctor, a lawyer, and a police officer; he forged checks, manufactured professional qualifications, committed other frauds, and routinely fabricated experiences (like escaping an airplane through the toilet drain). The movie, starring Leonardo Di Caprio, "Catch Me If You Can" is based on his life.

It is not permanent. It comes and goes, in varying degrees of intensity. While I maintain it cannot be 'cured', I do believe it can be controlled. You don't eliminate it, but you can alleviate it.

It's not a character flaw or a sign of weakness, or, as mentioned before, a mental illness.

It's not just a "women's issue." It's is not limited by gender, although the triggers and manifestations often differ between men and women.

It's not always evident to the person who is experiencing it.

It is not a superpower, and it should not be pursued or embraced or seen as a necessary element of the success journey.

That's a lot of "nots." So, what exactly *is* impostor syndrome?

Impostor Syndrome History

Google it. You'll get this: "It's the persistent disbelieve that one's success is deserved or has been legitimately achieved as a result of one's own efforts or skills; the condition of feeling anxious and not experiencing success internally, despite being high-performing in external, objective ways. It often results in people feeling like "a fraud" or "a phony" and doubting their abilities." The brevity of the description hides the multi-layered nuances of the experience. It's so much more of a journey than a moment. I would describe it as the chronic inability to feel great about being great, being unable to match your confidence to your competence, thereby limiting your influence.

Symptoms: Coping Strategies and Competence Types

As I mentioned before, Valerie Young is the co-founder of the Impostor Syndrome Institute, the world's leading source of impostor syndrome resources. Her 2011 book, *The Secret Thoughts of Successful Women: Why Capable People Suffer From the Impostor Syndrome and How to Thrive in Spite of It* is iconic. (To better reflect the more gender-neutral approach, the subtitle of the updated 2023 version was revised to "Successful Women and Men.") Her view on the topic is that it has been over-psychologized, putting excessive burden on the individual to "fix themselves." It is an individual experience, but there are circumstantial and situational contributions that cause people to feel like impostors, and when these contributing factors are fixed or at least considered, the impostor syndrome experience can be disarmed. I know this to be true, because this book changed my own life when I read it in 2014.

Young's book centers on expanding and applying these insights to real-world contexts, in professional settings. She offers actionable advice, anecdotes, and tools designed to help individuals recognize and combat impostor syndrome in their personal and professional lives. Her focus is on practical application and empowerment, making her work a valuable complement to Clance's foundational research. Unfortunately, Young's work is often plagiarized. Many people unknowingly and

Get Your Best People to Give Their Best Effort

inaccurately use her content without giving her the credit she deserves, leading to widespread misinformation and a lack of acknowledgment for her original insights and contributions.

Building beyond her book, she developed "Rethinking Impostor Syndrome" a program with a fresh approach that challenges the traditional view that impostor syndrome reflects a personal flaw and instead can be attributed to how external factors like societal expectations, workplace culture, and systemic biases contribute to these feelings of self-doubt. In this program, she explains that people with impostor syndrome tend to have unrealistically high expectations or definition of competence for themselves. The expectations fall into specific categories or types, and are evident by associated behavior or belief, which she calls "competency types." The five she explains are:

- **The Perfectionist:** I must strive for flawless performance 100 percent of the time.
- **The Expert:** I must know everything there is to know about a topic.
- **The Natural Genius:** Everything should come easy and fast. If it doesn't, I'm stupid.
- **The Soloist:** If I'm really smart, I should be able to do it alone, and do it first.
- **The Superhuman:** I must multitask constantly, perfectly and without complaint.

Building on the work of Clance and Imes, Young also describes patterns of behavior or "coping mechanisms" that help people both alleviate the fear of being found a fraud *and* prevent them from being found a fraud because they turn them into a rock-star employee.

In her book "Impostor Phenomenon" and in her clinical experiences with Imes, Clance identified telltale symptoms and coping mechanisms, including things like:

- Diligence and hard work
- Procrastination
- Being a first-generation professional
- Holding back, staying silent or "go along to get along"

- Using charm/humor/wisdom to deflect from a self-perceived lack of intelligence
- The need to be special or unique
- Inability to accept compliments, praise, and recognition
- Guilt about success
- The tendency toward introversion (although they may appear to be extroverts)

Young adds a few more:
- Flying below the radar (giving low effort and still producing acceptable work)
- Starting but not finishing projects
- The tendency to self-sabotage (substance abuse, frequent job changes, chronic tardiness, or causing conflict)

In my keynote, I summarize the symptoms, coping strategies and competency types into six categories:

- **The Impostor Cycle (as described by Clance/Imes):** of bouncing between over-preparation and procrastination, but still knocking the work out of the ballpark.
- **The Perfectionist**
- **The Superhero:** Doing things perfectly, and alone. Not delegating.
- **The Fascinator:** Using charm, wisdom, humor and personal style.
- **Fear of Failure:** The extreme aversion to the possibility of failure to the point they don't even start something.
- **Fear/Disdain of Success:** Not wanting success to change them; having weird issues with higher compensation or special treatment; Not certain of being able to repeat or sustain the track record of success.

That's a lot of information. It's easier to see it if we look at one person's journey.

3

Jan's Journey

In her book *Impostor Phenomenon*, Pauline Clance describes a cyclical pattern of behavior exhibited by most people struggling with this self-doubt. To illustrate how this looks in real life, let's meet Jan. She's an established professional with a great reputation in her industry and workplace. She has a degree from a wonderful college, has been in her industry for fifteen years, and with her current employer for about ten years. She is respected by her peers, and is considered a conscientious hard worker by her boss. She's easy to get along with, dependable, and produces great work. (By the way, Jan isn't a real person, but an avatar of the impostor syndrome sufferer.)

On the outside, Jan looks awesome…smart, confident successful. But inside her mind, it's a different story. Her professional journey has been an adventurous but sometimes tumultuous ride filled personal and professional ups and downs. People witnessed what she experienced and how she handled it, but her thoughts and feelings…she keeps those hidden. She was plagued with the self-doubt of impostor syndrome, and her journey looked like this:

Get Your Best People to Give Their Best Effort

Stage 0: The Comfort Zone
Her Experience: Getting her degree was challenging, but personally rewarding for Jan because she loved studying, researching, and learning. She was a good student with a solid GPA, and was able to land a job in her field. She spent the next few years enjoying the job. She gained a reputation in her industry of being easy going, competent and reliable.
Thoughts: "I'm good at this. It's become second-nature. I'm very comfortable here!"
Feelings: Secure. Confident. Strong. Proud. Self-assured.

Stage 1: Seed of Doubt
Her Experience: Jan was rewarded with a promotion. It was a new challenge with new responsibilities, higher pay, more influence, and greater visibility. Change usually triggers impostor syndrome.
Thoughts: "I'm excited, but why did they choose me? Do I have what it takes to do this new job? What is required of me now? What if I fail? What if my prior success was a fluke? What if I cause the company to fail? If I do okay at first, can I sustain it?"
Emotions: Initial excitement, a bit of anxiety, insecurity, fear of failure.

Stage 2: Drive and Mis-Drive
Her Experience: To handle the growing stress, Jan dove into the challenge, working hard to prove her worth (the "drive"). At other times, she procrastinated, opting for tasks that felt easier or more urgent, like research or waiting for feedback (the "mis-drive.") These tasks seemed productive but were actually creative ways to avoid the work she should be doing.
Thoughts: "I need to work hard to keep up! If I fail or make a mistake, everyone will know I'm not cut out for this, and will unmask me as a fraud. I can't ask for help…that will make me look incompetent. My entire career will look like a sham! I'm not sure how to start this project, so I won't. I'll clear my inbox instead."

Jan's Journey

Feelings: Stress, pressure, more anxiety, dissatisfaction in work, self-loathing for small mistakes, sense of inadequacy despite evidence to the contrary; shame at procrastinating. Isolation can creep in.

Stage 3: Triumph Time

Her Experience: In the middle of the drive/mis-drive cycle, Jan achieved something great, like solving a tough problem, hitting a huge goal, or overcoming some big obstacle. Whatever it was, everyone cheers!

Thoughts: "Whoa! That was close! They almost found out I'm a fraud. I got lucky. I had a lot of help from a great team. Everyone is overestimating my skills. They didn't see all the mistakes."

Feelings: Jan is puzzled by the praise and cannot relax. She's embarrassed by the attention, and feels guilty because it's undeserved. She's borderline humiliated because of obvious mistakes she made, yet relieved that people didn't figure out her true fraudulence. She feels shame that she really isn't what they think she is.

Stage 4: Rinse and Repeat

Her Experience: Tomorrow is a new day, and Jan will face a new challenge, new project, new responsibilities, new opportunities, and new expectations. The whole process starts over at Stage 1.

Thoughts: "Somehow I did okay. But what if I can't keep it up? They'll see I'm not qualified. Why are they so impressed with me? What's wrong with them? Can't they see I'm incompetent? I'm really stupid. I don't belong here. But I can't let them down. I can't let my guard down. Must. Keep. Working."

Feelings: Negative emotions continue to compound. Feelings of fraudulence are a constant companion. Coping mechanisms of overworking, procrastinating, isolating and multitasking are in full swing, giving the appearance of outstanding work ethic and superior skills, but she knows better, and feels out of integrity.

Get Your Best People to Give Their Best Effort

Jan, like many people, stays stuck in this process, where stage 4 reverts back to stage 1. This cycle needs to be disrupted. That's where you as the leader can step in. Understanding the sources and reasons for feeling impostor-ish is helpful.

4

You Mean I'm Normal?

There are a lot of Jans out there. I chatted with a friend who is a commercial pilot and had just been promoted to captain. That's a big deal in the airline industry, and he was excited. But he was also concerned. He said, "I know I'm a good pilot, but captain is a different level of responsibility. More pressure, for sure. I hope I can measure up." Despite being well-established and qualified, the promotion was messing with his head. I looked at him and said, "Yes, it makes sense. Impostor syndrome screams the loudest in times of change and transition, like a promotion."

I could see the relief on his face. It was as if he had his concerns validated, and it was okay to feel uncomfortable.

He should be okay with it. It's normal for career change to trigger doubts. In fact, there are many legitimate reasons besides change that can lead to feeling like a fraud. It hits certain demographics, certain industries, certain career paths. There are a variety of sources that make people more susceptible to it. You're more normal than you know.

Here are some of the most common reasons why perfectly capable and successful people can feel like an impostor, or question their capabilities. For this list, I've drawn inspiration from the pioneering work of Pauline Clance, Suzanne Imes and

Get Your Best People to Give Their Best Effort

Valerie Young, and then drew from my own experience and conversations with others. Yet, it's probably not exhaustive.

1. **Your upbringing.** We are a product of how we were raised. Your parents did the best they could, considering they were raised by people who did the best they could. Most parents don't have evil intent, but as a parent I know that even my best intentions were often clouded by poor judgment, bad moods, and exhausted frustration.
2. **As a child you were praised excessively or pushed to perform.** If your family prized good grades, outstanding athleticism or musical virtuoso, you may have been recognized for the outcome, not the effort. If you were celebrated for the mere act of breathing, and everything you did was extraordinary, you have a skewed idea of what is good performance.
3. **You carry a label from your past** (e.g., "the funny one" or "the slow one.") Childhood labels are hard to shake. They define us, and guide our actions. Going against the label starts to feel 'impostor-ish."
4. **You were supremely talented as a child**, maybe in sports, music, academics. A child I know had impressive hand-eye coordination from a very young age. As a toddler, he would throw a ball at a target and never miss. He later fell in love with Rubik's Cubes, speed stacking, yo-yos, and tennis…all requiring a crazy level of hand-eye coordination. But as he grew older, mastering things outside of that made him question his intelligence.
5. **You have a STEM background** (science, technology, engineering, and math.) Keeping up with new developments causes you to feel like you're always behind, especially if you are niched in a narrow expertise. Plus, you're convinced that others know more than you do.
6. **You work in a creative/artistic/performing arts job.** You're only as good as your last great artistic

product. You doubt you have what it takes to produce something amazing, again and again.
7. **You have a management or leadership role**, including C-level executives. Higher-level leaders have more responsibilities, more uncertainty, and less mentoring. It really is lonely at the top.
8. **You earned a credential, certification or advanced degree** (CPA, MD, JD, PhD, Financial planner, etc.) Advanced education is filled with impostor syndrome triggers, especially if you have to reaffirm and re-demonstrate your skills, with regular examination, recertification or licensing.
9. **You are part of a minority, underrepresented population or have a noticeable physical trait.** Any time you don't look, think, act, dress or sound like those around you, you'll feel out of place, and that's the start of impostor syndrome.
10. **You made a significant career transition.** Impostor syndrome screams the loudest in times of change.
11. **You're in the world of academia,** especially collegiate and above (professors, grad students, research assistants, etc.) The pressure to research, publish, secure grant funding is overwhelming. If you're at an elite institution, the pressure to compare and despair is especially powerful.
12. **You're a recent college graduate.** College is so different from real world employment. Related to #10.
13. **You must cross organizational/expertise lines in your job duties.** For example, you're a marketing expert in an engineering firm. It's like being in a foreign country, trying to learn the language. Or feeling like your education doesn't measure up to those around you.
14. **You're from a different culture, geographic location, education level or economic background** than your coworkers. See #9. Key word: different.

15. **You work in an organization that fosters competition and accomplishment.** If you're not a competitive person by nature, or motivated by prizes/awards, you'll always feel out of place in a competitive environment. If the corporate culture emphasizes outcome over effort, you'll stick to what's easy for you to accomplish, staying under the radar, never being able to be proud of your work because it didn't seem like a big deal to you.
16. **Your organization doesn't emphasize mentoring.** If you work well alone, that's one thing. But if you really need guidance, sounding board, coaching, direction and your organization doesn't provide it, you'll always feel like you have to figure it out yourself. You'll wonder if you're doing it right as you are doing it.
17. **You work alone.** With no outside influence, it's hard to judge how you're doing. You can't tell if what you're doing is right, and you're working in a vacuum. COVID really did a number on people in this area.
18. **You are an entrepreneur.** Related to #17, you may work alone, or from home, or be the person responsible for every aspect of your organization. Even if you have employees, the buck starts and stops with you, and you'll feel you need to know every aspect of everyone's job. That's a lot of knowledge, and a lot of pressure.
19. **You still struggle with finding the MUTE button.** If you repeatedly get tripped up with simple things or make the same mistake over and over, or are trying to adopt new strategies, it's normal to feel a period of adjustment. Call it that. Don't label it incompetence.
20. **You are human.** Self-doubt, making mistakes, experiencing change, feeling different from others, avoiding pain…it's a human thing, and nothing to be ashamed of. You're in good company.

You Mean I'm Normal?

Clearly, impostor syndrome is widespread, and it does not discriminate. A friend of mine runs a mastermind group for talented leaders and entrepreneurs. He invited me to give a presentation about impostor syndrome to his group. Weeks later, he texted me: "Wow! The group *still* talks about your session! They had no idea that they're not the only ones who struggle with it, and how even the best in the world experience it."

That's not surprising. In fact, the more accomplished you are, the more impostor syndrome can show up. Cheerful news, huh? On the flip side, the older you get the more adept you become at handling it. It's a paradox, but a pleasant one. I'd rather be an overcomer, than have nothing to overcome. Carol S. Dweck, an American psychologist renowned for her work in mindset and motivation, and author of the book, *Mindset*, says, "A hallmark of a successful person is that they persist in the face of obstacle, and often, these obstacles are blessings in disguise."

If you struggle with impostor syndrome, take heart! You can push through the obstacles and see the disguised blessing waiting for you. If you're a leader of people who struggle with it, I can think of no better way to lead and no greater reward than to lead people to push through obstacles and find their own disguised blessing waiting for them. They win. You win. It's win-win.

5

Locked Down and Shaken Up

Aside from these 20 legitimate and normal reasons to feel like a fraud, there's one more issue that demanded its own chapter.

COVID changed everything. If change brings on feeling of fraudulence and self-doubt, then it makes sense to address how the massive amount of change that occurred across the globe has affected the self-assurance of even the smartest and most qualified people. Let's look closer.

You probably recall certain events with crystal clarity. I recall the Miracle Mets of 1969 winning the World Series. The wedding of Prince Charles and Lady Diana. The Shuttle Challenger explosion (ugh…I was working for NASA at that time. It was such a difficult time in our agency's history!)

And of course, the 2020 pandemic. It changed so much about our world.

You would think that if change brings on impostor syndrome feelings, and COVID caused a lot of change, those impostor syndrome feelings would increase. Surprisingly, this was not the case. A UK study in 2020 revealed that impostor feelings dropped dramatically for people during COVID due to being forced to work remotely.

Valerie Young reflects on this: "Some people who experience impostor feelings find the isolation of working at home to be a relief because they can fly below the radar a bit more and therefore, avoid being—in their mind—found to be lacking, i.e. an impostor. In fact, some people might choose to work remotely precisely to avoid scrutiny." But for those who thrive on in-person, face-to-face contact it was awful.

COVID changed how business does business. The entire world shifted almost overnight, and left people scrambling to set up a home office, deal with Internet access, learn Zoom, establish processes and schedules to get their work done, all while juggling home chores, family dynamics, kids doing school from home, and the panic of a worldwide pandemic. What a mess.

Here's the paradox. Remote and hybrid workplace models can both amplify and diminish impostor syndrome. Consider how it amplified them first. Fully remote workforce model exacerbated impostor syndrome in ways that are categorized in two specific areas: Being at home, and being online.

Being at home

Isolation intensified loneliness and disconnection. When you're working entirely from home, you don't have the in-person experience. Gone were the random conversations in the hallway, or in the lunchroom. There was no more "meeting after the meeting" casual debrief after a conference room gathering. No more zipping over to your coworker's desk to ask a quick question. Newly hired employees did not to get to know the "vibe" of the workplace, or the subtle office dynamics and politics. Not having these organic interactions which are so important to human socialization can leave you feeling unsure of your place in the organization, which leads to feeling like you don't fit in.

Corporate presence changed. With no boss nearby, there may have been a lack of ongoing managerial presence in the middle of all the uncertainty. Where decisions were communicated quickly up and down a hallway of an office building, now it was a bit slower, via text, email, phone or zoom call. Corporate priorities shifted quickly during the pandemic, causing confusion, fear and discord, all of it experienced in isolation, not community.

Instant feedback was lacking. Without having a sounding board or a mentor close by or an ever-present supervisor or someone to answer a question in the moment, feedback is delayed. That perpetuates the anxiety of "Am I doing the right thing? Am I doing this thing right? Am I doing it fast enough or thoroughly enough?" Positive feedback or celebration at a job well done was so toned down. No high-five or hugs to recognize rewards or milestones.

Time and space boundaries were compromised. It was a challenge to find privacy, space, quiet, and access to resources needed to do the work while at home with family and pets and neighbors around. Having to balance family responsibilities, especially with children doing school at home was a colossal challenge. A person's private home life was exposed on video calls. Making a business phone call from the laundry room or garage or backyard to guarantee quiet made a lot of sense. People were having meetings and phone calls at all times, in all places. Hotels, airports, parking lots, the beach. Or, they found it easy to ease off, maybe call it a day earlier than normal, or multitask during their work by watching TV or playing games or doing chores. That led to feelings of guilt, especially if they felt like they weren't getting as much work done as they should.

Terminated employment and drop in income: Some lost their job or their revenue altogether. As a professional speaker, my revenue was wiped out when my speaking events were canceled overnight. Many of my speaker friends pivoted to providing virtual presentations, but for me, it was not an easy transition. To do virtual keynotes at a high level, you needed multiple cameras, microphones, switcher devices, lighting, monitors, a staff, and a different mindset. The technology confused me, and I felt stupid. I wanted to be a speaker, not a TV

Get Your Best People to Give Their Best Effort

producer. I did a few virtual programs with nothing but my laptop camera, built-in microphone, and a bright table lamp. Not only did I not like it, I thought my audience didn't either. I knew I didn't have the slick fancy setup that some of my speaker friend did, and I felt insecure. So, I quit speaking altogether. In the summer of 2020, I found a full-time job in my bucket-list industry: interior decorator and sales at a La-Z-Boy furniture store. I loved that job, and had it for two years until in-person meetings started roaring back in 2022. Then I quit La-Z-Boy and returned to keynote speaking. The transition to furniture sales was hard because I didn't have a design background, or a retail sales background, or a corporate organization background. But I was good with people, and the company was desperate for new employees. It was win-win for all of us even though my income dropped dramatically. Some income was better than no income, and I considered myself blessed.

Overthinking about one's performance: Spending so much alone can cause individuals to get stuck in their own heads overthinking things. Common recurring thoughts include:

"I worry I haven't been productive from home."

"I worry I'm not as prepared as I should be for the meeting or update."

"I worry everyone else has been more productive than me."

"I'm not sure I feel proud of the work I've done during the shutdown."

Being Online

Tech struggles: The most often repeated phrase of 2020 is "You're muted." Even the smartest people struggled to master Zoom. Virtual platforms were not new, but they weren't widely used until 2020. Not only was getting comfortable with the technology a challenge, getting accustomed to the physical actions of talking to a computer, looking at a screen with fifteen faces (including your own) looking back at you was just plain weird. Chances are that you were quite distracted by seeing yourself on video, and that was what you looked at most of the time. I know I did.

Online distractions: We got distracted by other people's backgrounds, including their pets, their wall decor, the books on their shelf, and the occasional family member who wandered around the background (usually fully clothed, but sometimes not.) We tried to mitigate it by using the green screen or background filters that made our heads look weird, and our hands disappear. We couldn't always figure out how to pin or unpin someone, and how to tell the difference between speaker view and gallery view. We had Zoom-envy of people who excelled in all those areas.

Personal connections suffered: Eye contact in a virtual meeting is impossible. If you look at the camera, you don't see other people's faces. If you look at their faces, they see you looking down or to the side and they feel unseen. Nobody wins. You can't read body language beyond facial expressions, and that's only if they keep their camera on. A lot of people choose to keep it off, creating an even bigger barrier to personal connection. Plus, with the camera turned off, it was so much easier to do something else, not even related to the work, which in many cases caused guilt and shame.

Group dynamics suffered: It was just way different on Zoom. In person, your head swivels and your whole body gets involved as you look from one person to another. On Zoom, only your eyes move, and while I can't point to science behind it, it feels less energizing and engaging. Chats helped, but reading one line at a time in a tiny box to the side of the screen is not the same as hearing a room full of conversation with vocal intonation, emotion and body language. Plus, once we all learned that the chat history can be saved, it made us all cautious of what we wrote, especially since the default setting sent chat comments to the entire group. Or to the last person who chatted with you. Or to the host. Actually, we rarely checked to see where it was going, and then were horrified when we found out. Ask me how I know.

Get Your Best People to Give Their Best Effort

Security issues created hesitancy: I've been Zoom-bombed by inappropriate meeting crashers sharing images I cannot unsee. Even after the software vulnerabilities were addressed, it was an uphill battle to get people comfortable using it again. Many companies went to alternate platforms, which meant people had to learn a new system all over again. Just when you get familiar with one thing and feel competent, it changes. Now you feel dumb again.

Overall, the pandemic created an environment where the usual support systems were disrupted, mental health issues rose and the pressure to perform was higher than ever, all of which exacerbated impostor syndrome.

Yet, that 2020 UK study tells a different story. Why did people feel less impostor-ish? Two sides to every story, indeed. The study highlights several reasons listed below.

Isolation limited social comparison because people were less likely to engage with coworkers outside of the meetings.

More autonomy over schedule, environment and effort led to increased feelings of competence and self-efficacy.

Without constant presence of managers and supervisors, many people were released from feelings of being micromanaged, leading to feeling less judged or scrutinized, freer to make mistakes or think outside the box.

Working from home can be more comfortable. No need to dress up. Your favorite food is close by, as is your comfy chair. Or bed.

With less emphasis on being present at their desk, and more focus on productivity and outcome, remote employees could feel more pride in a job well done. They feel valued for their contribution, not just physical presence.

Initially, the COVID shutdown posed major challenges for businesses transitioning to virtual operations. Over time, peoples' resilience and adaptability improved the situation. As of June 2024, most businesses have moved back to in-person work to regain collaboration and team camaraderie. In fact, the appeal of flexibility and work-life balance from virtual work has led many employers to adopt a hybrid workplace model.

Locked Down and Shaken Up

You've probably faced these challenges in your leadership duties, and you've likely tapped into the resources available to guide you through it. I won't repeat the strategies like "communicate your vision" and "set reasonable goals." I will, however, encourage you to evaluate for yourself the impact of remote or hybrid workplace model has on the well-being and productivity of your employees, balanced with the corporate goals and philosophy of your organization.

I repeat: understand first, lead second.

6

Men vs. Women?

Impostor syndrome knows no gender, but it does affect men and women differently. It's important to note too that while there are many perspectives on gender, this book will focus solely on the binary model as it aligns with my convictions, experiences and the bulk of the research on this topic. However, please know these are generalizations and not immutable truths—everyone's experience is unique.

When I give my keynote, I notice a distinct pattern in the conversations I have with attendees after I'm done. Women often want to confess their impostor syndrome and discuss their feelings of self-doubt and inadequacy. They seek validation and support, sharing their struggles.

On the other hand, the men in my audiences are more inclined to ask me about my NASA experience and share their own passion for space and aeronautics. There are some men who will talk about impostor syndrome, but it's not as many as the women.

This may seem to affirm the assumption that women experience it more than men. But that's not the case. Research into the differences along gender lines is inconclusive. Some

Get Your Best People to Give Their Best Effort

studies say they do, some say they don't. Men and women *both* experience it, but process it differently.

People's responses are shaped by societal norms, gender expectations, and brain function. Women are often conditioned to be more expressive, while men are encouraged to be stoic. Communication differences also stem from brain science, including neurotransmitters and language processing. While sweeping generalizations are just that, evidence from various fields still suggests that men and women do exhibit differences in how they respond and communicate.

For men, it often hides behind a mask of overconfidence and performance. You might find them taking on too much to prove themselves, while deep down, they might fear exposure as a "fraud." The famed entertainer, David Bowie told Q magazine in a 1997 interview, "I had enormous self-image problems and very low self-esteem, which I hid behind obsessive writing and performing… I was driven to get through life very quickly… I really felt so utterly inadequate. I thought the work was the only thing of value."

Women, on the other hand, often process impostor syndrome by questioning their abilities and holding themselves back from opportunities. They might hesitate to take on new challenges due to fear of failure or judgment or fear it will change relationships. "Will they still like me?" When I first considered applying for the promotion to the Facility Manager of the Propulsion Systems Lab, I froze. Despite having the experience and wanting the job, I asked myself, "Do I have what it takes? Can I do the job as well as my predecessor? What will my co-workers think? I'll be a level above them. Will they still like me? What will the PSL crew think? I'll be the first female and youngest person to have the job. Will they still respect me?" My internal self-talk was a very loud and stubborn push-pull, and I had to talk myself through it to get the courage to apply for the job.

In general, women tend to internalize their doubts and seek reassurance, while men often focus on external achievements and interests, perhaps as a way to mask or counteract their own insecurities. Understanding these gender-related responses can

Men vs. Women?

help leaders provide more tailored support to individuals grappling with impostor syndrome, fostering an environment where everyone feels empowered to succeed.

Confidence Gap

Claire Shipman and Katty Kay, in their book *The Confidence Code*, describe a confidence gap between men and women. Their work shows how women often underestimate their abilities, expect to underperform, and feel less deserving of advancement, even though they perform as well as men. In contrast, men tend to overestimate their abilities and feel confident even when they might not be fully competent, and will often take more risks.

You may have heard about a study done by Hewlett Packard, published in *The McKinsey Quarterly*, that states women will only apply for a job if they have 100 percent of the qualifications, and men will apply if they have 60 percent. For example, say a job description has five qualifications. A woman looks at it and thinks, "Hmmm, I can do #1, #2, #3...oops, I can't do #4. I'm out." A man looks at it and thinks, "I can do #1, #2, #3,...but not #4 or #5. That's 3 out of 5. I'm in!"

The problem is that there was no such study done. And while the gist of the story seems plausible, the reality is that it's not based on actual data. Hearsay evidence indicates it likely was born from a comment made in a conversation with a HP executive that somehow eventually rose to the level of research.

Does that negate the assertion that women and men incorrectly assess their skills? Probably not. I know for myself, the HP "study" sounds plausible to me. When I looked at the qualifications for the job of Facility Manager of the Propulsion Systems Laboratory, I saw some elements that I knew were shortcomings for me. I was tempted to bail out on applying for the promotion. I'm so glad I didn't.

Another way men and women differ is in their response to success and failure. In his 1958 book, *The Psychology of Interpersonal Relations*, Psychologist Fritz Heider lay the groundwork for "attribution bias" which is the tendency people have to attribute

Get Your Best People to Give Their Best Effort

behaviors and outcomes to either personal action/qualities (internal causes) or situational circumstances (external causes). With regard to impostor syndrome, it's fascinating. When men succeed, they attribute it to their own skills or prowess. When they fail, they attribute it to external things like lack of resources or poor team members. When women succeed, they attribute it to luck or timing or a great team. When women fail, they blame themselves.

Men internalize success and externalize failure. Women internalize failure and externalize success. No doubt any person's success or failure is some combination of both internal and external causes. But the attribution bias trap is hard to escape, and can have detrimental consequences in an organization.

For example, when someone *externalizes a failure*, they may fail to learn from their mistake because they don't even recognize their contribution to it. They may resist accountability or cast blame on undeserving coworkers. When they *internalize success* to the extent they take full credit for it, they'll undermine teamwork and collaboration, and create workplace tension. If someone *externalizes a success*, they can't be proud of their contribution or able to enjoy their success. *Internalizing failure* diminishes motivation and resilience, and can lead to isolation and poor team dynamics.

Bottom line: men and women tackle impostor syndrome differently. From how they talk to others, to their self-talk, to how they estimate their own skills—it's a mixed bag of societal pressure, gender norms, and brain wiring. Leaders, when you get this, it changes the game. Want your team to be self-aware? Walk the talk. Craft strategies specific for each individual. Impostor syndrome isn't one-size-fits-all. Recognizing these gender nuances isn't just helpful—it's your secret weapon in guiding your team past those nagging self-doubts to let your team's confidence soar.

7

The Impostor Test

In your journey to "Understand first" you may find it helpful to take the assessment below. Created by Pauline Clance, it is used as a measure of the level of impostor phenomenon feelings. It can also provide you a framework for the following chapters as you start to observe your team and develop your strategies to guide them through their own self-doubts.

Most people feel self-doubt or uncertainty at some point in their life. Does this mean they're all feeling like an impostor? No. Isolated self-doubt or occasional trepidation is part of being human, but there are other signals that, taken as a collective whole, do point toward this impostor experience. The following assessment quiz[1] can help determine if, and how strongly, you cross swords with this foe of fraudulence.

---

[1] (Note: This Clance IP test is from the book "The Impostor Phenomenon: When Success Makes You Feel Like A Fake" (pp. 20-22), by P.R. Clance, 1985, Toronto: Bantam Books. Copyright 1985 by Pauline Rose Clance, Ph.D., ABPP. Reprinted by permission. Do not reproduce without permission from Pauline Rose Clance, drpaulinerose@comcast.net, www.paulineroseclance.com.)

Get Your Best People to Give Their Best Effort

For each question, jot a number from 1-5 corresponding to one of these replies:

1: Not at all true

2: Rarely true

3: Sometimes true

4: Often true

5: Always true

Don't over-think. Give the first response that enters your mind, and then move on.

1. I have often succeeded on a test or task even though I was afraid that I would not do well before I undertook the task.
2. I can give the impression that I'm more competent than I really am.
3. I avoid evaluations if possible and have a dread of others evaluating me.
4. When people praise me for something I've accomplished, I'm afraid I won't be able to live up to their expectations of me in the future.
5. I sometimes think I obtained my present position or gained my present success because I happened to be in the right place at the right time or knew the right people.
6. I'm afraid people important to me may find out that I'm not as capable as they think I am.
7. I tend to recall the times in which I have not done my best more than those times I have done my best.
8. I rarely do a project or task as well as I'd like to do it.
9. Sometimes I feel or believe that my success in my life or in my job has been the result of some kind of error.
10. It's hard for me to accept compliments or praise about my intelligence or accomplishments.
11. At times, I feel my success has been due to some kind of luck.

The Impostor Test

12. I'm disappointed at times in my present accomplishments and think I should have accomplished much more.
13. Sometimes I'm afraid others will discover how much knowledge or ability I really lack.
14. I'm often afraid that I may fail at a new assignment or undertaking even though I generally do well at what I attempt.
15. When I've succeeded at something and received recognition for my accomplishments, I have doubts that I can keep repeating that success.
16. If I receive a great deal of praise and recognition for something I've accomplished, I tend to discount the importance of what I've done.
17. I often compare my ability to those around me and think they may be more intelligent than I am.
18. I often worry about not succeeding with a project or examination, even though others around me have considerable confidence that I will do well.
19. If I'm going to receive a promotion or gain recognition of some kind, I hesitate to tell others until it is an accomplished fact.
20. I feel bad and discouraged if I'm not "the best" or at least "very special" in situations that involve achievement.

Add together the numbers of the responses to each statement. If your score is:
- A total of 40 or less, you have few impostor characteristics.
- Between 41 and 60, you have moderate impostor syndrome experiences.
- Between 61 and 80, you frequently have impostor feelings.
- Higher than 80, you often have intense impostor experiences.

Get Your Best People to Give Their Best Effort

The higher the score, the more frequently and seriously the impostor syndrome may interfere in your life. It can interfere when the pressure of perfection, the disappointment of unreached goals or fear of a new challenge is too great. In the following chapters we'll dive deeper into the symptoms and signs of impostor syndrome, so you can recognize it within your team.

8

Be Like Mel Gibson

When Pauline Clance and Suzanne Imes initially identified impostor phenomenon, they noted a few of its critical attributes:
- The chronic fear of being exposed as a fraud;
- The belief that others overestimate your skills;
- The tendency to downplay your own achievements.

At the core is a thought-pattern distortion with massive negative self-talk that falls into some general and overlapping categories. Here are some common themes and thoughts they might experience:

Fear of Exposure:
"Is today the day everyone finds out I'm a fraud?"
"I'm going to be exposed as incompetent."

Downplaying Success and Accomplishments:
"My success was just a fluke."
"Anyone could have done it. I'm not that special."

Comparing to Others:
"I'll never be as good as everyone else."

Get Your Best People to Give Their Best Effort

"Who am I to be doing this job? Surely someone else is better for it!"

Perfectionism:
"If I don't do this perfectly, everyone will know I'm a fraud!"

"I'm representing an entire gender (or race or country or university or industry or fill-in-the-blank...) I can't screw up!"

Attributing Success to External Factors:
"I only did well because I had a great team."

"They must have made a mistake in choosing me."

Disqualifying Positive Feedback:
"They're just being nice. They don't really mean it."

"I don't deserve a raise or such a high salary."

Internalizing Failure:
"It's my fault."

"If only I had done _____ different, this would have succeeded."

Feeling Inadequate:
"I don't belong here."

"I still haven't mastered that skill! I'm stupid."

Refusing to Delegate:
"If I'm really smart, I shouldn't have to ask for help."

"How can I explain how to do this if I'm not sure myself? I'll just keep to myself!"

There is a cacophony of distress going on inside their heads. Yet, Impostor syndrome is a well-guarded secret, not one that people confess. I've seen it over and over: people walk into my conference session, timidly looking around. Once they see the crowd, their anxiety lowers and they think, "Whoa! I'm not the only one?" But verbalizing it is hard. After my keynote, I'll seek individual video testimonials from them about what they learned to use in my marketing. Getting people to talk on camera about a topic that is so personal, intimate and soul-baring is hard. Especially when they're thinking, "Oh my gosh. My boss is right there and now he knows I feel like a fake." Or, as I mentioned

Understand the Effect. Then Expect.

previously, the CEO who confided in me, "Wow...you were talking to me!"

Clance's and Imes' original 1978 research paper on Impostor Phenomenon confirms this hidden nature of impostor feelings. They reported that in their clinical experience, their clients initially presented with the normal things that drive people to therapy like anxiety, relationship issues, and depression. None of them showed up saying "I feel like an impostor." Those feelings weren't uncovered until after several sessions.

Today, impostor syndrome has become much more mainstream but it's still somewhat shrouded in secrecy and shame. As a leader, your ability to see past the secrecy, beyond the mask of competence will enable you to break the barriers to the brilliance of your team.

In the film, *What Women Want*, Mel Gibson gets the power to hear women's thoughts, giving him amazing insight into their behavior, leading him to connect more with them. Imagine if you, as a boss, had that kind of superpower with your team. You'd know what's going on in their heads—their worries, their ideas, their struggles. It would be pivotal for understanding and supporting them.

But the inner thoughts of a person with impostor syndrome are camouflaged by their outer world. They get a lot done. They take on challenges and new roles. They pursue excellence. They don't drain you. On the outside, they appear to be total rock stars.

It's easy to be lulled into thinking that because they're so reliable and good at their job, they require no attention. But if they're truly suffering with impostor syndrome, it's just a matter of time before their well-oiled, well-performing, well-dressed self takes the beating that come from chronic self-doubt.

What if you had a simplified guide for deciphering the connection between what you see in your team and what they are likely thinking? Wouldn't it be cool to channel your inner Mel?

When we met Jan in chapter six, you saw how thoughts and emotions lead to actions. Here is your "Translation Guide" to see

Get Your Best People to Give Their Best Effort

how your coworker's actions, as indicated by the symptoms we discussed in Jan's chapter are reactions to their internal thoughts.

Your Translation guide
Because what you see is not what they think!

Impostor Cycle	
What you see	**What they think**
• A total rock star team member. • Smart, diligent, efficient, reliable, flexible, competent, creative.	I didn't sign up for this. This is not what I expected. The stress is getting to me. I can't let on how I really feel. I'm terrified I'll be found out as a fraud. I'm not as smart as they think I am. They think I'm competent, but I feel like an idiot.

The Over-Preparer	
What you see	**What they think**
• Thorough preparation, long hours, many meetings, lots of emails, exhaustive research, frequent status updates. • Seek constant affirmation and validation for their work. • They double- and triple-check their work. • Won't take much time off. • Often will not delegate.	• I'm not sure what work to do, so I'm going to do all kinds of work because somewhere in there is the right work. • I must know all details of this project if I'm going to be effective. • I need more information, time or money. • Providing more detail shows I am really on top of things. • It's not done till it's overdone. • Shortcuts are not allowed. • I must be prepared for every situation. • Can I really trust others to do their job?

The Fascinator	
What you see	**What they think**
• Personable, witty and the life of the party. • Like to converse about past interesting projects. • They share wisdom and fascinating trivia. • They are often well groomed, well dressed, very fit and fashionable. Or edgy and funky. • They name-drop, or seek to hang with people of influence or power.	• If I keep them laughing, they won't notice I'm not smart. • If I share fascinating tidbits of information, they'll think I'm smart. • If I look good, I am good. • If I hang with cool people, I'll be seen as cool. • My best days are behind me, so I'd better talk a lot about it. • My past accomplishments prove I'm worthy. • Be charming! Crabbiness is a character flaw.

Understand the Effect. Then Expect.

The Procrastinator

What you see	What they think
- Initial enthusiasm for new role, followed by long period of easygoing inactivity, finishing with massive activity to complete the work. - Often will underestimate time needed to complete the work. - Can be indecisive, but will mask it with "research and prep" activity. - Easily distracted by easier, lower-priority tasks. - They may have a reputation for delaying work and affecting team dynamics. - Produce quality work. - Will often defend their incomplete work by deflecting blame.	- I'm not sure how to start, so I won't. - I did it well last time, but I don't know if I can do it well again. - What if I start the wrong way, and have to change midstream? That's a disaster. - Measure twice, cut once? No, I'd rather measure a hundred times and cut none. - I'm just not motivated. I'm sure I'll be more motivated tomorrow. - It's too big a project! - I need more training. I'm not qualified to do it yet. - I need more certifications. Then I'll be able to do it. - There's not enough time today, so I'll start first thing tomorrow. - I don't know why I'm procrastinating! I feel like such a loser. - If I talk about it a lot, they won't notice I'm way behind on actually doing it.

The Perfectionist

What you see	What they think
- Will rarely admit a lack of knowledge. - Make few mistakes, and won't tolerate mistakes in others - Want more resources to make it better. - Don't accept praise well. - Quick to point out flaws in their work - Never seem to enjoy the outcome because it's not good enough. - Appear humble, noble and disciplined - Detail-focused. - All-or-nothing thinking.	- Flaw = Fail. - If I make a mistake, I AM a mistake! - If I make a mistake, they'll see I'm not smart! - Only the outcome matters, not the effort. - I don't care what it costs or what is sacrificed. The only thing that matters is that I'm seen as perfect. - I'm better than everyone else, but I try to pretend I'm not. - I must highlight my perfect accomplishments and hide all flaws. - I should have done better. - They think I did a good job? Didn't they see that mistake?

Get Your Best People to Give Their Best Effort

The Super Hero

What you see	What they think
• They juggle a LOT of priorities well. • They don't delegate, ask for advice or seek help. • The get a ton of work done. • Don't mentor others well because they take over. • They over-promise, AND over-deliver. • Are held in high esteem by coworkers. • They're often the "go-to" person on the team.	• If I say no, they'll think I'm weak. • If I'm smart, I shouldn't need to ask for help or advice. • If I delegate, I'd have to explain what I need and I don't know exactly how to explain it. • How hard can this be? I can do it. • If I delegate and they fail, that makes me look bad. • Others are too busy to help me. I don't want to bother them. • I can't let go of the control. It makes me feel special, useful, respected, and influential.

Fear of Failure

What you see	What they think
• They don't volunteer for risky assignments. • They are often compliant, and won't challenge the status quo. • They voice objections by framing them as "What if _____ happens?" • They are pessimistic. • Their complaints are masked as concern. • They suck up resources with constant rechecking and reviewing. • They isolate and withdraw in groups and meetings. • Let others make decisions and take the lead. • They see feedback as a character attack. • Can overlap with the perfectionist, over-preparer and the procrastinator.	• Failure feels like death. I won't survive. • Winners never fail. • Failures never win. • Failure is final. • If I fail at even a small part, I've failed at the whole thing. • No failure or flaw is acceptable. • I don't think I can do it well, so I won't do it at all. • I can't be trusted with an important project. I'll blow it. • Who am I to be doing this? • How can I ensure zero failures? • My ideas are dumb, so I'll keep silent.

Understand the Effect. Then Expect.

Fear of Future Success	
What you see	**What they think**
• Steady-Eddie, dependable and predictable. • Slow to embrace change, apply for promotion, or take credit for successful work. • May engage in self-sabotage like poor time management, disorganized work area, substance abuse, chronic lateness. • Great starters, but terrible finishers. • They may refuse promotions, citing it will negatively impact their family or affect their personal relationships. • Lack vision/goals • Have a hard time celebrating other's promotion and improvement.	• If I succeed, will I be able to sustain it? • I succeeded once. I don't think I can do it again. • If I continually start new things, I'll always look busy. So what if I never finish? Someone else can pick up where I left off. • I didn't think this would be so hard when I began. I'll start something else and figure this out later. • I need more education or certification. Then I'll be ready. • If I get promoted, will I have time for the things I love to do? • Will my coworkers like and respect me if I get promoted? • She'd be much better at the job than me. I'll step aside and let her take it.

Disdain Current Success	
What you see	**What they think**
• Struggle with work-life balance. • Discount their own contribution to success. • Attribute success to others. • Respond to praise with "Oh it was nothing." • Make lots of self-deprecating comments. • Point out the flaws in their work that nobody else notices. • They shrink back from a new challenge after experiencing success. • May express disdain for higher salary. • Lack long-term goals. • Very humble, to the point of being annoying.	• It was a total fluke! I got lucky. • I got the job because I know the right people. • I have no idea how I got here! I could lose this at any moment! • A monkey could do this job. • Wow. I must have really fooled them into thinking I could do this. • There's nothing special about me. • I was in the right place at the right time. • I feel so guilty getting this salary! • I can't handle this stress. I wish I was a nobody. • If they only knew I don't know what I'm doing!

Of course, this is not an exhaustive list, but you get the picture. There is a lot of thinking going on under the facade of superior performance. Undoubtedly, the high achiever on your team is having some of these internal dialogues. Maybe you are too. Thankfully, you (and they) don't have to stay there!

9

Impostor Syndrome and Intelligence Theories

The process or the product?

I love sewing. I've been a sewist for over fifty years. (By the way, "sewist" is what we sewing fans call ourselves. A "seamstress" is a one who sews professionally. A "sewer" is where dirty water goes. I'm neither of those.)

I get lost in the process of sewing. But by the time I'm done with a project, whether it's a dress or a pillow or jammies for my kids, I'm tired of what I'm sewing and I want to start another project. I love the process more than the product. But then, there are others who love the product more than the process.

Interestingly, this somewhat parallels intelligence and learning theory as described by Stanford University Professor and Psychologist Carol Dweck. According to her, there are two intelligence models on the continuum of implicit beliefs: fixed mindset and growth mindset. People with a fixed mindset (also called "entity theory") believe that success is based on innate

Get Your Best People to Give Their Best Effort

ability and a fixed entity of unchangeable intelligence. People with a growth mindset (also called "incremental theory") believe success is based on effort, learning and disciplined commitment to improvement. Growth mindset rewards effort and discipline. Fixed mindset emphasizes outcome and performance over effort. Process vs product.

At first glance both seem noble, and both have their own benefits. People with a fixed mindset can develop specialized proficiency in something because they have a natural talent and "it just comes easy." They stick to what's easy and what they're good at. They may develop a strong sense of security and stability because of familiar surroundings and predictable outcomes. They often will develop more efficient ways to do their work, even creating shortcuts, which make them productive and creative. They reduce the risk of failure because they maintain more control over their work, tasks and outcome. They tend to set and measure their worth with outcome (product) goals.

People with growth mindset also flourish, but in different ways. They embrace challenges and setbacks, seeing them as opportunities to grow. Resilience is their hallmark. They are motivated by growth and improvement. They are more open to new ideas, take more risks, and are champions of innovation. They have a more positive outlook, devoid of stress or anxiety. They value lifelong learning and self-improvement and strive to make positive changes in their personal and professional life. They are often optimistic and confident, enjoying the process of growth. They embrace the statement "success is a journey, not a destination." They tend to set and measure their worth with process goals.

Of interest is the link between mindset and the accuracy of a self-assessment of one's own skills, something often skewed with people experiencing impostor syndrome. At the heart of impostor syndrome is the inability to see oneself as talented and skilled. On the surface, this seems like a fixed mindset, the idea that one cannot learn beyond a certain level. However, the opposite is true. In her book *Mindset*, Dweck explores this issue of inaccurate self-assessment of one's abilities. She references

Understand the Effect. Then Expect.

work done by University of Michigan Professor of Psychology, David Dunning (originator of the Dunning–Kruger effect) that indicate people with a low ability in a specific area give overly positive assessments of this ability. We've all seen examples of this on televised talent shows like American Idol. The crummy singer gets a "no" from the judges, and then gets infuriated with them for rejecting what is "clearly" exceptional talent. This version of over-estimating one's skills was due to a combination of low skill as well as a low level of self-awareness. They didn't know what they didn't know.

That's not what interested Carol. She wanted to see if there was a link between mindset and the over-estimating. She observed that most of the over-estimators actually have a *growth* mindset. On reflection, it makes sense. Growth mindset people are more open to feedback about their skills, and accurate information about them even if unflattering, is beneficial to them as they strive to grow, improve and stretch themselves. The difference between the growth mindset over-estimators and the "American Idol" over-estimators is self-awareness that led to a very different level of personal humility and lasting change.

However, both fixed and growth mindsets can have dark sides, showing up in maladaptive behaviors that create toxic environments.

People with **fixed mindset** will tend to avoid challenges or changes, which limits opportunities for growth. They don't just fear failure; they don't think they have the ability to learn something new, so they won't even try. They see negative feedback as personal criticism, so they'll often not accept coaching, mentoring, training or advice. They are their own worst critic, filled with harsh self-talk and negative self-image, especially when surrounded by people they perceive to be more talented or successful. After a setback, because their resilience is low, they'll give up. They limit learning because they don't see the value of it, leading to stagnation and low achievements. In their relationships, they often struggle with communication and conflict resolution because they believe personality traits are unchanging and it's fruitless to overcome the differences.

Get Your Best People to Give Their Best Effort

The dark side of the **growth mindset** is just as shady. These folks may be more overconfident or arrogant, willing to take on challenges for which they are not prepared. Sometimes their resilience is short-lived, and fades in the face of extended challenges. Their continuous learning and improving can mask procrastination which delays taking action. Their strong focus on self-improvement and drive for perfection can backfire and create situations like burnout, disappointment, and soured relationships.

Mindset pendulum

While both growth and fixed mindset have their pluses and minuses, it's the extremes that can cause the real problems. In *Mindset*, Carol Dweck describes a few notable leaders that, despite being regarded at one time as very successful, were actually stuck in a fixed mindset that led to the demise of their business and reputation. Lee Iacocca of Chrysler, Albert Dunlap of Scott Paper, and Kenneth Lay, the founder and CEO of Enron, didn't mean to do harm, but were so myopic in their vision and their influence, they didn't notice that the ship was sinking.

Refusal to learn a new skill because of a stubborn belief in one's singular skillset or unique intelligence could be a significant roadblock. For example, when the COVID shutdown started, college professors found themselves in an extremely challenging situation. Having spent 6–9 months preparing a year's syllabus, they had to quickly pivot (the word of the century) to online classes. They had to learn virtual technology, online presentation skills, strategies that keep students engaged, learning management systems (LMS), and how to mimic the more organic community that is fostered in person on campus.

Data confirmed the struggles. In April 2020, Cengage conducted a survey across 641 US higher education institutions about their priorities during the COVID shutdown. The results revealed that 97 percent of institutions used faculty with no prior online teaching experience. Almost half of the faculty surveyed wanted more information about how to transition to online learning. Almost 60 percent wanted webinars for their students to learn how to succeed with online learning, indicating that the faculty themselves were not equipped to prepare their students as well as they would like. Almost half the faculty (48 percent) lowered their expectations about the amount of work students would be able to do, and almost as many (46 percent) dropped some exams or assignments.

In early 2020, my son and daughter were both enrolled in two different universities, and my oldest brother was teaching math at a third. It was fascinating to compare their COVID experiences. My daughter was a freshman studying film, and thought one of her professors dropped the ball regarding transitioning to online learning. My son was a physics student, and fell behind because critical lab classes were canceled. He was discouraged and considered changing majors, but did choose to continue. My brother is one of the most popular instructors at his university. He admits to not being tech-savvy at all, and while he struggled to learn the online platform, he was committed to it so he could deliver the best education to his students. He did it, despite often being exhausted and overwhelmed.

Do these data and anecdotal situations reflect fixed vs growth mindsets of higher education students, faculty and administrators? Maybe. Maybe not. But the extreme of refusing to adjust to changing circumstances certainly has far-reaching consequences.

Mindset changeability

A growth and fixed mindset can exist simultaneously in the same person. A person may have a growth mindset about their ability to learn a new language, but a fixed mindset about their musical ability. Mindset is affected by external circumstances as well, such as the company we keep, the type of feedback we get, and even the temperature of the room we're in. Work environment and relationships can shape mindset. A supportive encouraging environment can foster growth, collaboration, innovation. A critical, competitive environment can cultivate risk-aversion, fear of failure, and a compare-and-despair vibe.

Get Your Best People to Give Their Best Effort

Focusing on outcome over effort, where checking a box is more important than the journey of becoming something great will create a pecking order of carrot-stick mentality that stifles innovation and fosters murmuring and complaining.

Mindset can also shift over time. Age and life experiences may influence mindset, but it's not a simple linear relationship. Younger individuals often have more malleable mindsets because they are in formative stages of development, exposed to new ideas and experiences. They might be more open to adopting a growth mindset if they are encouraged to learn, take risks, and view failures as opportunities for growth.

As people age, their mindsets can become more fixed, influenced by life experiences, successes, and failures. Older individuals might hold more entrenched beliefs about their abilities and potential. However, this doesn't mean that a growth mindset can't be developed later in life. With conscious effort, reflection, and the right environment, people of any age can shift toward a growth mindset.

Some studies suggest that older adults may benefit more from adopting a growth mindset, as it can lead to greater resilience, improved cognitive function, and enhanced well-being. In 2022, at age sixty-one, I took up ballroom and Latin dance. I have no background at all in dance, but I was willing and eager to learn. Here I am, more than two years later, performing and even competing in amateur contests. I wish I had done this sooner!

What does this have to do with impostor syndrome?

There are several parallels between mindset concepts and the impostor syndrome. Fixed mindset and impostor syndrome both manifest as self-doubt, sensitivity to feedback, and a fear of failure. Growth mindset can be an effective approach that promotes resilience, healthy response to feedback and more openness to challenges.

You'd think that people with growth mindsets would not struggle with impostor syndrome. Despite the dark side of the growth mindset that could morph into or mimic impostor

Understand the Effect. Then Expect.

syndrome, it sounds so...mature, so...growth-y. Surely they don't struggle with impostor syndrome, right?

And you'd think that fixed mindset people *would* struggle with it more. Someone who believes that their intelligence cannot change is likely to make a determination of their own capabilities and then fail to change that assessment even when they succeed at something. They may explain it away as luck or timing. They will feel out of place when surrounded by people with more education or experience or talent. They won't ask for help, thinking they must do things on their own. So, surely the fixed mindset folks feel impostor syndrome, right?

Yes and no. Actually, while impostor syndrome is a heavily researched and documented subject, research around the relationship between this self-doubt and intelligence theory (mindset) is both lacking and contradictory. Some studies confirm a positive correlation between growth mindset and higher impostor feelings. Some don't. A 2021 study by Sydney Vian at the University of Wisconsin LaCrosse examined the relationship between mindset and the impostor syndrome. The hypotheses was that people with a fixed mindset experience more impostor syndrome, but the study results did not support that. In contrast, a 2005 study by Dr. Shamala Kumar and Dr Carolyn Jagacinski of Purdue University did. However, because the study subjects (i.e. the people studied) were not completely apples to apples, a true comparison is not possible.

The maladaptive behaviors of the dark sides of both the growth and fixed mindset can easily emphasize one's impostor syndrome experiences. Based on the description of some of the symptoms in an earlier chapter, it's easy to see how someone with *either* a fixed or growth mindset can feel impostor-ish. Consider these comparison examples:

Because a person with a *fixed mindset* believes their abilities are static, it leads to a false conclusion that any shortcoming or failure reflects a lack of ability. This can lead them to "feel fraudulent" in the face of success, especially if they attribute their success to luck or timing, instead of inherent ability.

Get Your Best People to Give Their Best Effort

A fixed mindset person sees feedback as a personal attack, not an opportunity for growth. Similarly, a person with impostor syndrome interprets negative feedback as a confirmation of their own perceived inadequacies.

A fixed mindset person pursues a perfect outcome; a person with impostor syndrome also pursues perfection, but their standards of success are so unrealistically high they never can truly enjoy the result because they always think "It could have been better."

A growth mindset person likes learning new things, but if impostor syndrome is present, they may find that learning something new is harder than they expect, and they'll think, "Why is this so hard? There must be something wrong with me."

A growth mindset person who embraces effort and persistence may be a person who starts a zillion projects but finishes none, leading them to feeling like a failure or a fraud.

A person with growth mindset who is overly focused on continually improving may feel constant pressure to prove their worth with evidence of continual growth. This can lead to feelings of inadequacy or failure if growth goals are missed.

A leader with a fixed mindset may harshly punish or judge a subordinate for making a mistake, and assume they're incompetent and not able to learn more. It can also lead to a feeling of superiority over those who are "less skilled."

A leader with fixed mindset may be so focused on successful outcomes desperate to prove their own worth by it that it causes them to make decisions about the entire organization that benefit only him/her, not the organization or people in it.

What does this mean to you as a leader?

It's tempting to say, "I want a team with a growth mindset!" because it appears preferable. Again, it sounds so "growth-y". And a quick internet search will be filled with blogs, comments and research that clearly favors growth mindset over fixed. Who wouldn't want a team of resilient, high-achieving, lovers of learning?

Understand the Effect. Then Expect.

However, having a balanced approach that recognizes the strengths (and dark sides) of each mindset could be more beneficial. This encourages individuals to leverage them based on the situation. This balanced perspective can lead to greater overall effectiveness, well-being, and success in various aspects of life.

The question isn't "Which is preferred, a fixed or a growth mindset?" The better question is "How do I lead people, regardless of mindset, to reach corporate goals, maximize my team's potential, and cultivate a robust organization?" That's a lot. Because going back to the sewing analogy, do you favor the product or the process in your organization?

How can you lead them? You influence them. Influence is just another word for leadership. Influence is organic but powerful, and sometimes the most powerful influence is unplanned, unchoreographed and unexpected. You can lead them by influencing their mindset, which will influence their impostor syndrome.

Success leaves clues. So does mindset.

By observing your team's behaviors, reactions to challenges and their approach to learning new things, you can see the clues to identify whether they're operating with a fixed or growth mindset.

Do you have any of these *fixed mindset* folks in your team?:

The Change Challenger: Their favorite statement is, "We've always done it that way."

The Responsibility Refuser: "That's not my job." Or "I'm not trained for that." A reluctance to take on different responsibilities could indicate a hidden fear of failing or being found incompetent.

The Defense Dynamo: "I had a lot on my plate that day!" or "I guess you missed all the other work I did right!" Someone who jumps into negative emotional defensiveness when getting constructive feedback could mean they view the feedback as a personal attack instead of an opportunity for growth.

Get Your Best People to Give Their Best Effort

The Green-eyed Grumbler: "She's the owner's cousin. Of course she got a good review." Or "He didn't really deserve the promotion as much as I did." Instead of celebrating other's success or being inspired by it, they choose to be envious or threatened by it.

The Effort Evader: "I'm not ready for that level of responsibility." Or "Someone else more qualified should take over. I'm afraid I'll mess it up." If something is too hard to do, they assume they don't have the natural talent for it, and they'll bail. They attribute success to inherent talent instead of effort.

Do you have any of these *growth mindset* folks?

The Challenge Champion: They love challenges and view them as opportunities to learn and grow. They say, "Bring it ON!"

The Bounce-backer: When faced with setbacks, they are resilient and persistent, seeing it as a temporary obstacle and learning opportunity rather than a defining character flaw.

The Yearn to Learn: They want to grow and develop, and go out of their way to do it.

The Feedback Cravers: They seek out constructive feedback, viewing it as helpful, not judgmental.

The Praise Promotor: They not only celebrate other's success, but they are also inspired and motivated by it.

If you want a team of growth mindset people, but find you have a lot of fixed mindset folks, there's still much you can do to influence them. You can employ strategies such as

- Asking them about their attitudes on topics like learning, challenges, and feedback.
- Use the information to cultivate a unique environment of growth and collaboration tailored to them that includes judgment-free sharing and community support.
- Evaluate your own growth mindset. Model for them what you'd like to see by embracing challenges and learning new skills.

Understand the Effect. Then Expect.

- Provide clear and specific feedback that focuses on effort and strategy that led to an outcome, not just the outcome itself.
- Recognize and reward hard work and progress, not just the goal itself.
- Quickly address negativity and conflict to prevent it from harming the organization's productivity, relationships, and bottom line.
- Establish continuous learning and development opportunities.
- Conduct training, hire consultants, provide coaches.
- Bring in outside experts who can educate and inspire your team to move beyond impostor syndrome, and adopt a growth mindset.
- Explore how to cultivate more teamwork and collaboration.

Above all, craft a comprehensive vision for your team and obsessively communicate it clearly and consistently. Highlight each team member's role in achieving this vision because when they understand their place in the bigger picture, they will recognize their value and be more committed to the vision. (This will be covered again in chapter 12.)

10

Understand the Effect. Then Expect.

Understanding mindset is important, but don't lose sight of the ultimate truth. I've stated this before: The single most significant thing holding your best people back from giving their best effort is not lack of talent, or lack of motivation, or lack of training. It is impostor syndrome. And it's costing your overachievers their peace, their pride and their productivity.

Your best people may LOOK like they're doing their best work. In fact, they probably are, but they're paying a price you cannot see. They are struggling with overwhelm, guilt, pressure, and doubts. They are holding back truly epic performance because they don't believe they have it in them to perform. In many cases, they're settling for "good enough." They've let the "good enough" become the enemy of the best.

Here are some specific situations in which it can arise:

Leading a critical project: with high stakes, high budget, high pressure. Despite having experience, that project leader may doubt their ability to deliver.

Performance review: Even great performers may still say to themselves, "Yeah, but…" or they dismiss the praise, or credit others to appear humble. Or, they may become defensive at constructive feedback, viewing it as confirmation of their incompetence.

Presentation anxiety: Many people dread public speaking. But for experts with impostor syndrome, the dread is accompanied with intense fear of being exposed as an impostor in their field.

Interacting with, presenting to or reporting to higher-level leaders, especially executives: Being around more experienced people in authority can be nerve-wracking, causing them to feel pressured to make a good impression. Despite lots of preparation, they may still feel their ideas are not significant enough.

Recently promoted: They may wonder if they deserved the promotion, if they can handle the new responsibilities, and how the promotion will change existing coworker relationships. This is especially true if they are promoted to be a direct supervisor of those coworkers. They will also feel pressure to be seen as *the* expert of the group, with more knowledge than everyone else, an unrealistic goal.

Networking events: Interacting with industry experts at a conference or client site can bring on impostor feelings as they compare themselves to others. It will silence them, hold them back, or prevent them from participating.

The Corporate Effect

Impostor Syndrome not only affects individuals. It affects the entire corporation or organization as well. For example:

Employee retention suffers: People with impostor syndrome can feel so anxious or undeserving of their role, they'll jump to another company to avoid "being found out."

Employee engagement goes down: If it's not practical to change jobs, they'll remain where they are and their

Understand the Effect. Then Expect.

dissatisfaction will grow into disengagement, dissatisfaction, absenteeism, and quiet-quitting.

Rewards/recognition issues: Impostor syndrome causes people to refrain from advocating for themselves because they don't feel they deserve the extra recognition. They often don't get the compensation they deserve, and may choose to stay "under the radar" leading to more shame or dissatisfaction. It can also undermine the reward system itself if less deserving or less qualified people who do advocate for themselves get rewarded or compensated.

Productivity suffers: When some people take on an inordinate amount of work to prove their worth, it can lead to burnout, absenteeism and presenteeism. Additionally, it spills onto the attitudes of their less diligent teammates, who may be okay to sit back and let the hard workers work hard, missing out on opportunities to contribute their full potential. Everyone loses, and the group productivity suffers.

Stifled innovation: A person who is not convinced of their skill will be much less likely to contribute a possible solution to a problem because they fear ridicule. They'll be less likely to engage in brainstorming, speak up in meetings, or point out hazards, flaws, or things to improve.

Health care costs increase: Quantifying the exact dollar cost to a company is difficult because there are so many direct and indirect factors. But no doubt, impostor syndrome costs money. For instance, the World Health Organization (WHO) estimates that depression and anxiety alone cost the global economy $1 trillion per year in lost productivity. It's not a stretch to interpolate that a portion is related to the anxiety and depression of impostor syndrome. Presenteeism in particular leaves employees vulnerable to added illness or extended recovery, further increasing health care costs.

Skill gap: Due to their self-doubts, employees with impostor syndrome will be reluctant to apply for promotions or move into leadership roles. This leaves positions unfilled, looking like a skill gap, forcing managers to look outside the organization. This leads

Get Your Best People to Give Their Best Effort

to more costs for searching, recruiting, onboarding and training new people.

The Personal Effect

While the corporate impact of impostor syndrome is significant, the toll it takes on individuals is also important to understand. Here's how impostor syndrome affects employees on a personal level.

- They experience guilt at saying no.
- They're uncomfortable describing their skills, abilities, and achievements.
- They avoid or disdain competition.
- They have an *intense* aversion to the possibility of failure.
- They don't give themselves permission to have an "off day."
- Saying "I don't understand. Can you explain that to me?" is not part of their dialogue.
- They're isolated. And it bugs them.
- They hesitate to interrupt someone and ask help, even in dire situations.
- If they're part of an underrepresented group, they feel pressure to represent that entire group.
- They may feel guilt for trying to prioritize interests outside of work.
- They feel pressure to keep up a façade of competence.
- They're unable or unwilling to identify their contribution to their success or the team's success.
- They're exhausted, scared, intimidated, and uncertain.
- They're your rock stars, stalwarts, steady-eddies, and high-performers. And that's what makes it so hard to lead them! They often lead themselves.

It's like identifying the cancer before you see the signs. And when you see it, you can't unsee it; you must address it. When

Understand the Effect. Then Expect.

move towards mitigating impostor syndrome, you can get your best people to give their best effort.

You think your team is great now? It can get so much better!

What to Expect

When your team members are released from the clutch of the impostor syndrome, they can expect to:
- Embrace the reality of their capability and potential.
- Be comfortable with taking risks when they realize it will not destroy them.
- State with appropriate pride, "I am a creative, intelligent, and influential person that has so much to offer."
- Silence the voice that speaks to them on the edge of a great challenge, sneering, "Who do you think you are?"
- Verbalize their expertise, with no shame, dismissal or apology.
- Learn to release the exhausting obsession with perfectionism without compromising their commitment to quality.
- Be free to invest into other's lives without feeling any additional pressure, obligation or manipulation.
- Define success in their own terms.
- Stop feeling stuck or invisible.
- Believe they smart and accomplished.
- Stop settling for lesser roles, lower status, and easier tasks.
- Stop being intimidated by people who appear to be more successful.
- Teach what they know to others, and delight in the process of sharing their expertise.
- Never fear being unmasked as a fraud or fake.
- Find deep internal satisfaction and joy in their career
- Stop wondering, "Do I measure up?"
- Enjoy the fruit of their hard work.

Get Your Best People to Give Their Best Effort

- Live with bold and courageous enthusiasm.

Now that sounds like a leader's dream come true.

11

Response to Success and Failure

In chapter 6, "Men vs Women?" I discussed externalizing and internalizing success and failures. This difference cannot be overstated, because success and failure are such touchy subjects for people with self-doubt. Your ability to guide them through it can be transformational.

I know failure. Early in my project engineer life at NASA in PSL, I was responsible for recording engine exhaust nozzle temperatures using a collection of three infrared (IR) imaging cameras, essentially night-vision cameras. At the time, this technology was cutting-edge, and the equipment was *outrageously* expensive. To protect them from hot engine exhaust, we housed the cameras in protective and cooled boxes, with a thick glass portal window. We constantly monitored the box temperature from the control room during testing. However, during one test, hot engine exhaust leaked into one of the boxes and the camera melted. It was a fluke accident, and no one saw it coming.

I was mortified. I was responsible for the system, and I failed. How did I miss this? How could I have made such a stupid mistake? If only I were smarter, or more experienced! We reviewed the series of events leading up to the incident, and we

Get Your Best People to Give Their Best Effort

saw evidence that in hindsight gave a clue to what would happen. But it only made sense looking back. Yet, I felt like an idiot for missing the signs.

I internalized the failure. I blamed it on my shortcoming, my failure, and my character flaw.

That's ridiculous. The mistake was not stupid. It wasn't even a mistake. It could have happened to anyone under similar circumstances. In fact, a dozen other intelligent people were in the control room with me, and we all missed it. The technology was so new, none of us were experienced enough to see the warning signs. Yet, in my mind, it was entirely my fault because of my flaws.

When people with impostor syndrome "make a mistake," it's a billboard announcement about their shortcomings, as well as a loud statement about their inability to evade discovery. They didn't just make a mistake. They *are* a mistake. It becomes their identity, and it haunts them. I dragged that oppressive feeling around with me at NASA for a very long time. I was terrified to step into the control room after that. I thought everyone labeled me as "the one who destroyed the IR camera system."

To compensate, I worked even harder at PSL. Our team replaced the damaged camera, and then devised better boxes to protect all three. The next time we ran the cameras during a test, I was hyper-vigilant. Halfway through that test period, I declared, "We need to shut down the test facility now so I can inspect the cameras. I want to make sure they're okay." I had no reason to suspect damage, but I was terrified of making the same mistake twice. The crew looked at me like I was a kook. "Maureen, you do realize it will take over two hours to shut down the engine, shut down the support machinery, open the test cell, open up the camera boxes, close the test cell, and bring everything back on line, right?" Yes, I was aware. Mid-test shutdowns are a colossal interruption and huge manpower drain. But I insisted.

Gosh, I was nervous. Would we find another destroyed camera, or would we find everything intact? A destroyed camera meant another failure. Intact cameras meant I was being overly

Response to Success and Failure?

cautious and irrational. Still, I felt I had no choice, and with the lead test engineer's permission, we shut everything down.

The cameras were fine. They stayed fine for the rest of the months of testing. The mountain of data we collected was valuable, showing trends never seen before. At the end of the project, people celebrated my work.

But I couldn't enjoy it. I replied with, "Well, it wasn't really me. I had a great team. And we collected good data only because the cameras were protected. Anyone could have collected this data." I didn't *internalize* the success. I *externalized* it. I wasn't convinced that I was capable of producing success on my own. Any success had to be the result of something outside of me, namely a great team and a better box.

I'm thankful that in our gritty, industrial research and development world of PSL, we had the attitude of "Fix what's broken and move on." Stuff was always breaking. It was the nature of our testing business. Nobody ever blamed me for the incident. The bosses were understanding. They valued my part on the team, and they got me back in the game. Good thing they did, because it could have gone south pretty badly for me as a young engineer who loved her job. I would have forever been "the girl who couldn't make it as a test engineer." I would have felt I let down my entire gender, and I think that would have crushed me.

This tendency of internalizing failure and externalizing success, referred to as "pessimistic-explanatory style" is linked with increased stress and even depression. In 1988, noted psychologist Martin Seligman coauthored an article in the *Journal of Personality and Social Psychology* titled, "Pessimistic Explanatory Style Is a Risk Factor for Physical Illness: A Thirty-Five-Year Longitudinal Study." The article describes a study that explored the relation between health and the tendency to explain success or failure on either external or internal circumstances. A person with a pessimistic-explanatory style habitually attributes bad events to causes that are stable (unchangeable), global (ever-present), and internal (self-sourced). He concludes, "Although mechanisms remain to be investigated, it is clear that the person who habitually explains bad events by stable, global, and internal

Get Your Best People to Give Their Best Effort

causes (I failed! It's my fault!) in their early adulthood is at risk for poor health in middle age." That's a high price to pay. It's consistent with what Drs. Clance and Imes observed with their clients that lead them to uncover this whole impostor experience in the first place. Those clients felt a high pressure to perform, and internalized every failure.

If you have people in your team that internalize failure, especially younger or newer people, you can encourage them to flip it around. Identify the external contributions to the failure that are not on their shoulders or in their character, and point it out to them. Emphasize it's not all their fault, and have data to support it. For example, suppose Steve, a new team member was responsible for leading a project that didn't meet its deadline. He could easily internalize the failure, thinking it's a reflection of his abilities and character. But you, as his leader, can flip his perspective. You might say, "Steve, I understand you're feeling down about the missed deadline, but let's look at the bigger picture. The delay wasn't entirely on you. The supply chain issues and unexpected software bugs were significant factors that were out of your control. You managed everything within your reach exceptionally well, and that's what matters. Look at the data. Your problem-solving skills helped us avoid even bigger delays. This situation doesn't define your abilities; it's a learning experience, and you're doing great."

However, here's a caution: this externalizing of failure can look a lot like *blaming*, so it's important to recognize the difference. *Blame* implies existence of malicious intent or character flaw, and the failure could or should have been avoided if they had a pure intent or better character. *Externalizing failure* seeks to define a reason not related to a person's action or lack of action. It does not attribute any malicious intent. It points to circumstances, environment, and glitches in technology. Accidents happen. Even if their actions caused the failure, remember that their worth is not defined by what they do. *Failure is an event, not a person.*

The reverse is true for success. For people on your team who externalize success and cannot own their contribution, your role

Response to Success and Failure?

is to produce the evidence of competence. Clearly identify their role, actions, decision, and results. Stress the link between their work and the outcome. Do not accept their minimizing perspective of it. It's not prideful or boastful to own up to your talents.

Imagine another team member, Alexis, who just led a successful product launch. The launch exceeded all expectations, bringing in significant revenue and positive customer feedback. However, when praised for the accomplishment, she downplays her role, saying, "I was just lucky; the market was ready for this product."

As a leader, you can show her how to recognize her contribution. "Alexis, this success wasn't just luck. Let's break it down: you identified a key market need, proposed the innovative features that set our product apart, and led the team through a tight development timeline. Your strategy and decision directly created this outcome. This success wasn't an accident. You made it happen."

By presenting clear evidence of Alexis' role in the success, you encourage her to internalize her achievements and build self-assurance. *When people internalize their successes, they can enjoy them more.* In the words of Thomas Jefferson: "I'm a great believer in luck and I find the harder I work, the more I have of it."

12

Is This a "Woo-woo" Topic?

No, it's not. But it may appear that way. Hang with me.

Impostor syndrome stems from distorted thinking but also has personal, emotional, and spiritual components. As spiritual beings in physical bodies, we experience life through our senses, intellect, and emotions, often on autopilot. We only notice our bodies when something heightens our senses or causes pain. We notice our emotions when we're emotionally stirred by something, like watching a favorite sports team win or missing an important deadline.

Our spiritual capacity is unnoticed until triggered by profound experiences such as tragedy, loss, joy, or love. Neuroscientist Dr. Daniel Amen, in his book, *Healing the Hardware of the Soul*, discusses how brain activity research shows we are wired for transcendental experiences. He highlights the temporal lobes as central to our emotions, desires, and spirituality. Studies by Andrew Newberg at the University of Pennsylvania show changes in monks' brain activity during meditation, indicating a link to euphoria and physical awareness.

Other research suggests that thinking about God can alter brain activity, hinting at a "God-module" in our brains. British

Get Your Best People to Give Their Best Effort

researcher David Hay found that 75 percent of people have had transcendental experiences, feeling connected to a higher power or sensing a greater purpose in life. These spiritual experiences, whether religious or not, are often long-lasting and life-changing.

What Does This Have to Do with Impostor Syndrome?

I wrote about this extensively in my book, *Pushing Your Envelope: How Smart People Defeat Self-Doubt and Live With Bold Enthusiasm*. Impostor syndrome highlights shame, an intensely intimate and powerful experience that is common to every human being. Shame differs from guilt. Guilt is objective and behavior-based, saying, "I made a mistake," while shame is subjective and identity-based, saying, "I am a mistake." To distinguish them, consider whether you broke a rule (guilt) or failed to meet a standard (shame). Guilt can be resolved through forgiveness and reparation, a self-directed activity. Shame requires unconditional acceptance, a gift of kindness and favor, usually from outside ourselves..

Brené Brown's research shows shame causes self-doubt and relational disconnect. Her "Shame Resilience Theory" suggests recognizing shame, identifying its triggers, and sharing your story to receive compassion and empathy. This approach relies on others' acceptance, which can be risky.

Self-acceptance is another approach, but it requires a reliable standard of worth. Dr. David Burns, in *Feeling Good*, outlines four unique paths to improved self-esteem: pursuing satisfaction, recognizing inherent worth, correcting distorted thinking, and treating oneself with deference and self-love. However, these methods can fall short without a dependable source of perfect standards and acceptance.

A Better Approach

True relief from shame comes from a transcendent spiritual experience, which some call grace. This acceptance can't come from other people, or even from within you—it must come from beyond you, such as from a higher power. The most powerful weapon against self-doubt is finding this external source of acceptance. We all long to feel worthy, but often hide behind shame. Recognizing your worth to and from a greater, external source allows you to contribute more freely to the world.

Brian Houston, in his book *For This I Was Born*, contrasts two similarly skilled businessmen: one focused on building his personal wealth and the other focused on funding church missionary work. The wealth-builder vision failed under pressure, while the mission-minded vision thrived because it was tied to a bigger cause. Houston emphasizes that a vision linked to something greater than oneself has the power to endure tough times.

Helen Keller said, "The only thing worse than being blind is having sight but no vision." Having a cause that is bigger than you helps override impostor syndrome fears. It shifts your focus from self-doubt to helping others. The most important causes connect, serve, or benefit other people. Replacing self-condemning thoughts with uplifting, other-focused ones creates a powerful, positive shift.

The Two Levels of Cause

At a personal level, finding a cause or mission that stirs you is a key to feeling fulfilled and resilient. It gives you a sense of purpose that goes beyond everyday struggles and self-doubt. When you connect with a cause that matches your values and passions, it boosts your motivation and keeps you committed, even during tough times. This mission becomes your guiding star for you to make decisions and take actions that are more impactful.

At the organizational level, it's your role to communicate a compelling organization cause and mission. When team members see how their roles fit into this bigger picture, they feel more connected and driven. But for this to work, the organization's mission needs to resonate with every team member's personal

Get Your Best People to Give Their Best Effort

goals. Leaders should make sure the mission is clear, inspiring and specific. Even if the vision is considered radical or socially controversial, it will draw the right types of people *you* want in the organization. When your mission matches with their principles, they join your journey. With the right people on board, everyone feels a sense of belonging and shared purpose, success and satisfaction multiplies.

To give you some framework, here are some examples of value and mission statements that are clear, intended to not only project corporate perspective, but to be a billboard sign to attract like-minded employees with a deep-seated like-minded focus:

Herman Miller, the iconic furniture manufacturer, operates on principles rooted in the founder D.J. DePree's Christian faith, attracting employees who value integrity and ethical business practices.

The shoe company, TOMS, is committed to social responsibility and giving back, attracting employees who are passionate about philanthropy and ethical business.

The mission of eyeglass provider, Warby Parker, is to offer designer eyewear at a revolutionary price, while leading the way for socially conscious businesses.

Mike Lindell, founder of MyPillow, is known for his Christian principles and resilience against cancel culture. The company's mission is: "To promote Christian values and resilience in the face of adversity."

Patagonia, the outdoor clothing and gear company, is committed to environmental issues, clearly stated in their mission: "Build the best product, cause no unnecessary harm, use business to inspire and implement solutions to the environmental crisis."

If your company mission is not clear, specific, and compelling, you may still attract good people, but they may be less-than-perfect-for-you people. You'll be tempted to want to change them, instead of lead them. Don't give into that. Crystallize your mission, and give the ones who want out a smile, handshake and some kind words. Let them go. It makes room for the right people who will align with you not just at the skill level, but the deeply personal transcendent and even spiritual level.

13

The Dreaded Skill Gap

In addition to finding workers who align spiritually with your mission, you now have to contend with a variety of abilities. Maybe this has been your experience when you were tasked with promoting or hiring someone. With a job opening to fill, you look at your team and see people who are qualified and people who are not. However, unbeknownst to you, impostor syndrome causes the qualified ones to not believe in their abilities, so they don't apply. On the other hand, those who appear unqualified might possess the necessary skills but haven't demonstrated the courage or initiative to prove it. The manager concludes, "I have more than a skill gap. It's a skill canyon! I must look elsewhere!"

You decide to look outside your team for a qualified candidate. You develop the job posting, collect applications, review resumes, conduct interviews, and whittle down to top three, conduct more interviews, and select someone. Then you invest time and money to onboard, orient, and train them. All the while, you hope you made a good choice and that they will like the job and stay. This process is costly and risky!

There's a better way. Let's break it down like this. First, look at your team. They probably fall into one of four categories:

Get Your Best People to Give Their Best Effort

A. Go-Getters: People who are qualified and do apply.
B. Reluctants: People who are qualified but don't apply.
C. Long Shots: People who are not qualified but do apply.
D. Stay-Puts: People who are not qualified and do not apply.

You really want the Go-Getters (the A's) to apply and the Stay-Puts (the D's) to not apply. Right? But what if what you see a lot of Reluctants? Or a lot of Long Shots? No Go-Getters. And you're kinda thankful for the Stay-Puts to just stay put.

However, you may want to look again. It's possible that your team members are far more qualified and capable than you think. Your Reluctants need some encouragement to be convinced of their qualifications. Your Long Shots and Stay-Puts may need further assessment before you dismiss them.

Over the past few years, Caterpillar, the famous world leader in construction, mining, and industrial equipment implemented restructuring plans to lower operating costs in response to sluggish global sales. A key element of their plan was job consolidation. Leaders wanted to survey their workforce to see how jobs could be combined, eliminated or revised. They decided to use a self-assessment approach where employees rated their own skills. After the results were compiled, employees would be given two options: A) train to gain 2–3 new skills and stay with the company, or B) leave the company.

It was fascinating how employees assessed their own skills. Most either overestimated or underestimated themselves. Studies show that self-assessments are notoriously inaccurate. People overestimate their skills out of ignorance. They are not bloviating or boasting. It's usually that they either don't know the skill level needed to perform a function or they don't know the outcome standard that defines success. It's the "How hard can that be? It's not rocket science!" or "Done is good enough!" approach. When these skill *over-estimators* are given new assignments, it soon becomes clear they're in over their head. The solution is simple: retrain or reassign…again.

The Dreaded Skill Gap

The bigger problem is with the people who *underestimate* their skills. Some of your Reluctants are qualified, but they don't think they are. But some of the Long Shots also underestimate themselves. Even if they want to advance, they undervalue themselves and assume that they lack skill or knowledge. They feel an internal tension, torn between "I want that promotion!" and "I don't think I'm qualified." Their internal voice says, "Don't try. It's too hard. You'll fail, and you'll be humiliated. Or you'll succeed, and you'll have to sustain the success…it's too much pressure!" It's the classic impostor syndrome, where that internal voice is sentencing a capable person to a life of chronic self-doubt.

The result? The Reluctants miss out on promotions and sweet assignments because of fear of failure. The Long Shots are overlooked for promotions because they don't give enough evidence to managers that they are indeed qualified or have the potential (or even the desire) for a different assignment.

It's Not a Lack of Confidence!

What looks like a **skill *gap*** is actually a **confidence *cap***. Cap, not gap. In other words, it's not a lack of confidence. It's a *limit* of confidence. These people have confidence…it's what got them where they are. They took the class, earned the diploma, applied for the job, showed up for the interview, accepted the job…all these things require confidence. But over time, they reach a limit of their confidence and stonewall themselves from moving forward. They silently suffer, and you assume you have a skill gap. Or a skill canyon.

As a leader, your job is to *remove that cap*, which will *close that gap*. To do that, it helps to understand the relationship between normal and occasional lack of confidence self-doubt and the chronic self-doubt of impostor syndrome.

They're different. A person can have lack of confidence self-doubt without feeling like an impostor. A little self-doubt is normal. But the one who suffers from impostor syndrome

Get Your Best People to Give Their Best Effort

compounds the limit of confidence with a disbelief in or dismissing of their capabilities and accomplishments.

Years ago, I stood at the top of a black diamond (expert) ski run at Telluride Ski Resort in Colorado. I'm a strong intermediate skier, but not an expert. I stared down a terrifying near-vertical drop and thought, "There's no way I can ski this! I will die. But I needed to get down the mountain fast to meet with my friends. I could take that easier path over there, but that's two miles long and it will take too much time. My only choice is this black diamond." My internal dialogue tormented me. "Could I ski this? I'm a strong skier but I've never skied anything like this. This looks hard!"

I was experiencing a normal self-doubt, which was legitimate. I was hesitating because in all my skiing experience, I had never skied on a slope this steep.

I stood there with the tips of my skis cantilevered over the edge. Suddenly, I made a choice. I leaned forward and launched myself down the hill. In a heartbeat, I was careening down the black diamond, scared out of my mind. I drew on every skill I could, focusing on keeping my skis parallel and my hips moving, shifting my weight, using my poles for stability, controlling my speed, and avoiding other skiers. My thighs and my lungs burned! All I could think was, *"Don't wipe out! Just do what you know how to do!"* It was intense and harrowing. It seemed like forever, but it was probably less than a minute before I was on much flatter terrain.

I stopped, turned around and looked at the slope I just tackled. To me, it looked like a wall, fifty stories high. "Wow! I just skied down THAT???? Did I just do that? There's no way I did that! I'm sure it was ugly! I got lucky!"

Impostor syndrome is the same thing: you doubt the truthfulness of what you accomplished.

This is the key difference between normal lack of confidence self-doubt and impostor syndrome: Before and after. Self-doubt stops you *before* you launch. Impostor syndrome goes with you *after* you launch. I could have taken the longer, easier run instead. But I didn't. I recall I felt terrified as I careened down the slope,

The Dreaded Skill Gap

saying to myself, "I don't know if I can do this!"..*.while I was doing it!* Clearly, I did know how to do the very thing that I thought I couldn't do. I didn't do it with the style and beauty of a true expert skier, but I got down the hill.

The Impostor is not the person who says, "I don't think I can do this." It's the person who says, "I'm not sure I'm doing this correctly now" while they are doing it. And then looks behind and says, "It wasn't all that great. I didn't do a great job. In fact, it wasn't me who did it. I got lucky."

In short, normal self-doubt *stops* you from stepping forward. Impostor syndrome accompanies you *after* you step forward.

Understanding the difference between this normal self-doubt and impostor syndrome self-doubt can help you encourage your Reluctants and Long-Shots to launch themselves over the cliff. If they're self-evaluating their skills, you may want to consider looking again at their past behavior to see if they've chosen the easier path, or have tackled the black diamond.

The normal self-doubt comes and goes. The real demon is the self-doubt of impostor syndrome where you discount both the truth and value of what you did. That will haunt you and rob you of joy. It helps to reframe when you accomplish something that challenged you, your symbolic "black diamond run." Turn around and say, "Yes, I did it. It may not have been pretty, but I did it, and it was a great ride. Best of all, I know I can do it again. And I'll keep getting better at it!"

14

Impostor Syndrome Is NOT a Superpower

There's a narrative floating around about impostor syndrome being a good thing. *Harvard Business Review*, *Forbes Magazine*, and the Bloomberg.com website all published articles about it. Well-regarded researchers and influencers like George Mason University professor Tyler Cowen, Adam Grant, a psychologist and professor at Wharton School of Business at University of Pennsylvania, and well-known author and motivational speaker Darren Hardy have each written about the "benefits" of impostor syndrome.

I have a different perspective. I don't think it's good at all. I don't want people to seek it out, or embrace it, or stop being told they have it. But these contrary perspectives still pop up.

So, let's play a little "point-counterpoint."

1. Impostor syndrome can drive personal development.

Nope. People seek personal development because that's who they are. They are of a growth mindset, are lifelong curious learners, and are buoyed by achievement. With or without doubts, they'd still work hard. In fact, character traits such as curiosity, optimism and persistence are a significant factor in battling impostor syndrome.

2. Impostor syndrome makes you work harder to prove yourself and gain the skills needed to succeed.

Nope. You can't fake a strong work ethic or a hunger for knowledge. Sometimes a person may push to learn something or work hard, but that doesn't mean they're trying to prove themselves. And even people who don't experience impostor syndrome work hard to gain skills and knowledge.

3. Having impostor syndrome fosters empathy toward others who experience it, creating a more supportive community.

Sorta nope. Empathy and compassion are developed over a lifetime through self-aware introspection and spiritual convictions. They're not triggered by a sense of inadequacy, and in fact, are suppressed by it. Impostor syndrome is rooted in shame; until that is addressed, you'll stay paralyzed and feel inadequate. Once you address your impostor syndrome, then you'll create a more supportive environment, because you'll be released from the angst, and able to be more involved with the people around you.

4. Impostor syndrome makes people seek help from others, leading to more professional growth.

Sorta nope. People with impostor syndrome don't ask for help because they think, "If I was smart, I should be able to do it by myself." Until they see this as a fallacy, they will not delegate or ask for help, no matter how much encouragement they get. And even then, asking for help will still feel like a massive leap of pride-swallowing faith into an abyss of uncertainty and unfamiliarity. It's hard, but it's worth it.

5. People can use impostor syndrome to their advantage to achieve more.

Nope. I'll repeat this again. The single most significant barrier preventing people from reaching their greatest potential and giving their best effort is not a lack of confidence, or lack of opportunity. It is impostor syndrome. It masquerades as other issues like boredom, burnout and high turnover. In fact, recent data from a NerdWallet survey of UK Executives reveal that "…59% of respondents had either thought about leaving or had left their job due to impostor syndrome, with an additional 31% considering doing so but not yet following through."

I don't see any of that as good. I'd much rather see people do the work to get through impostor syndrome than simply live with it. It is way more fun, rewarding, and constructive.

6. Impostor syndrome pushes you to work harder and avoid boredom, and is the psychological fuel required to perform at greater heights.

I agree and disagree. Humans naturally seek stimulation and purpose. Lacking that, we feel bored. Boredom pushes us to find satisfying activities that release dopamine, giving us pleasure and purpose. Boredom triggers curiosity, industry and movement.

However, the converse is not always true. Not all curiosity, industry and movement is driven by boredom. Some is driven by a person's personality trait, a desire for personal growth, or goal of financial gain. Some people are just industrious and curious, hardworking and eager to learn.

There's also the difference between resting and being bored. Resting involves taking a break to relax and recharge. It's a deliberate and beneficial activity aimed at recovering energy, reducing stress, and improving overall well-being.

Being bored is a state of mind characterized by a lack of interest, excitement, or engagement in one's current activities or surroundings. Boredom often arises when there is a desire for stimulation or something more engaging to do but nothing readily available meets that need.

The key difference lies in motivation. Boredom-driven activities alleviate discomfort, often without a tie to goals or values. In contrast, industriousness-driven actions reflect natural diligence, align with interests and values, and are fueled by an internal need for achievement and growth.

In essence, resting is intentional and rejuvenating, while boredom is unintentional and uncomfortable.

Moreover, the brain's chemical response to boredom-driven activities differs from that of goal-oriented or industrious activities. Various neurotransmitters and hormones—such as dopamine, serotonin, endorphins, and adrenaline—are released in different quantities depending on the stimulus (i.e., boredom or goal-oriented activities). This varied chemical release can lead to distinct psychological and physiological reactions. In other words, the relief one feels when alleviating boredom is not the same as the satisfaction of achieving a goal or overcoming a fear.

Impostor syndrome and boredom are polar opposites. People that experience impostor syndrome do work hard, but they're hard workers by nature, not people trying to battle boredom. If they experience guilt when taking a rest, that's a different issue altogether. Life-work balance and prioritizing personal leisure and mental health is something they should take a closer look at.

I caution against implying that impostor syndrome is good and unavoidable. It's not. Left unchallenged, it harms mental health and leads to chronic stress and burnout. Don't pursue or embrace it. Instead, acknowledge it, and then stamp it out. **It's a trigger for change, not a requirement for change.**

I invite you to encourage your team to develop a healthier approach of challenging their thoughts, celebrating their achievements, and learning from their failures. Adopting a better strategy that balances wins and lessons (not wins and losses) creates a well-rounded lasting way to combat impostor thoughts.

15

Jan's Journey: After

Back in chapter six we met Jan, who was stuck in the four stages of the impostor syndrome journey. To recap, the four stages are:

Stage 1: Seed of Doubt
Something changes (such as job, role, life circumstances), which triggers self-doubt thoughts and feelings of insecurity.

Stage 2: Drive and Mis-drive
Coping strategies such as overwork and/or procrastination alleviates fear of being unmasked as a fraud. Stress and anxiety lead to exhaustion, shame and isolation.

Stage 3: Triumph Time
Despite the fear, she is a rock star! Everyone cheers. She thinks, *"Whew! That was close! They almost found out I'm a fake!"* She cannot relax, and picks apart the flaws, which heightens her secret shame.

Stage 4: Rinse and Repeat

A new day comes with a new challenge or project, and the whole cycle starts all over again.

If you're committed as a leader to making a difference, you can most definitely disrupt and reroute Jan. What if Stage 4 were followed by a new "off-road" path for Jan and everyone like her? It would look like this:

Stage 5: The Light Bulb (aka Enlightening Epiphany)

Experience: Jan hears, reads or sees something about impostor syndrome that stops her in her tracks. She sees others who seem to enjoy success, but she also meets others who feel like she does. She knows her health has deteriorated, and she must change something. She begins to recognize the pattern of impostor thoughts and starts questioning their validity. (Plot twist: You can facilitate this light bulb moment.)

Thoughts: "Why do I always feel this way? You mean, I'm not alone? There's a name for this? And a way through it? I'm in!"

Feelings: Exhausted from overwhelm; frustration gives way to curiosity, self-loathing leads to self-awareness, and a perpetual dissatisfaction morphs into an intense and hopeful desire for change.

Stage 6: The Exploration for Options

Experience: Jan dives into researching impostor syndrome to find ways to alleviate it, and change the outcome. (Plot twist: You can facilitate this too!)

Thoughts: "I'm going to Google it. Wow. There's a lot of content out there, a lot of blogs, books and research. I didn't know this."

Feelings: Hope, relief, anticipation, optimism, curiosity.

Stage 7: The Rethinking

Experience: Jan is jazzed! She implements what she's learned. She's more aware of how experiences create thoughts which cultivate feelings, which drive actions. She begins to see that having different thoughts can result in different actions, which will have different outcomes. She changes her inner self-talk. She sees setbacks as opportunities. (Plot twist: You can model this and facilitate her reframing.)

Thoughts: "I'm learning so much about how I process situations, thoughts and emotions. I *am* as smart as everyone thinks I am. I may not know everything, but I don't need to. I have an accurate assessment of my skills and abilities. I've worked hard to create my success. Was there luck or timing involved? Yes, but I still did the work to create the outcome. It's okay to make mistakes and learn from them. It's also okay to ask for assistance or advice."

Feelings: Empowered. Healthy pride. Self-acceptance. Reduced anxiety

Stage 8: The New You

Experience: Jan is different. She stands tall with self-assurance and determination. Her smile is genuine and warm, reflecting her inner peace and self-acceptance. She showcases her personality and confidence with a stylish and comfortable appearance. She engages with others openly, offering support and encouragement, and she embraces new challenges with a positive growth mindset, knowing her worth and capabilities. Her presence is inspiring, embodying resilience and the triumph over self-doubt.

Thoughts: "I'm living with purpose. I engage with those around me, I'm authentic. I have a lot to offer, and I know I am good at my job, and I enjoy it! I'm surrounded by people who I can count on, and who count on me. I'm free from the pressure of being perfect. I am ready for challenges, growth, and celebrating my victories."

Feelings: Confident, resilient, optimistic, content, curious, bold, free, focused, authentic, inspired.

Imagine having an entire team of Stage 8 Jans. This journey is not always linear; individuals may move back and forth between stages. Overcoming impostor syndrome involves continuous self-

Get Your Best People to Give Their Best Effort

reflection, seeking support, and developing strategies to manage and diminish these feelings.

But what if you are the one who struggles with impostor syndrome? I'm glad you asked.

PART TWO: LEAD SECOND

"If you want to build a ship, don't drum up the men to gather wood, divide the work and give orders. Instead, teach them to yearn for the vast and endless sea."

-Antoine de Saint-Exupery

16

When the CEO is the CEI

As you delve deeper into understanding impostor syndrome and its impact on your organization, you might find yourself thinking, "Hmmm...I think I have impostor syndrome. I'm not just the CEO, I'm the CEI...Chief Executive Impostor. Ouch." Relax. It makes perfect sense. The higher up in an organization you go, and the more success you experience, the more impostor syndrome appears.

Data confirms this. An article on March8.com in December 2022 included survey results stating 78 percent of business leaders feel impostor syndrome at work, and a whopping 60 percent of them considered leaving their job because of it. That's awful! Far too much is at stake, and too many excellent leaders are not convinced of their competence. Other surveys from organizations including Blind, Olivet Nazarene University, Fedora Training, and others all point to the same conclusion: a significant percentage (from 58 percent to 75 percent) of leaders and executives struggle with impostor syndrome. Execs and tech leaders from Amazon, Microsoft, Google, and Facebook have experienced impostor syndrome at some point. Entrepreneurs

Get Your Best People to Give Their Best Effort

and startup founders feel it. Male, female, young, established…all feel it.

So, exhale. You're not alone. You're not broken. But you do have the edge, because recognizing this is a crucial first step to leading your team.

And even if you don't struggle with impostor syndrome, as a leader, it behooves you to understand it. As Valerie Young says, "If you lead, manage, teach, mentor or parent others, you need to understand impostor syndrome!" Who knows? You may find some very useful ways to address regular self-doubts that come at you from time to time. Or maybe you'll see that you experience some aspects of impostor syndrome more often than you'd like. It doesn't matter. When you make it a priority to understand it and apply it to you first, you'll have more compassion, more understanding, and the boldness to change your culture making impostor syndrome a reduced threat in your workforce. Plus, when you address it in yourself first, you'll have an advantage over other leaders who don't. You'll get to your own goals faster.

Adopting these strategies for yourself won't just help you in your career. You'll be so much more in tuned with the world around you. You'll be a better spouse. Better parent. Better chef. Better golfer. Better dancer. Better party guest.

You'll be proud of your past accomplishments but not in an obnoxious, prideful way. You'll be able to embrace your success in a way that reflects the specialness you bring to the world, without discounting or dismissing it. You'll feel great about being great.

Matt Clark, a former NASCAR champion pit crew leader is now a mindset coach and business strategist. In an interview with host Robert Eisenstadt on the Bad Beat Podcast, he reflected on his life's journey:

"I spent a lot of years at NASCAR, and because of my background, I didn't feel like I belonged. I only played community college baseball; I coached at a small Division 3 college, and all of a sudden, BOOM! I'm at the top levels coaching the pit crews, for Jimmy Johnson and Jeff Gordon. I worked hard to get there, but there was still something in the

When the CEO is the CEI

back of my brain saying, 'Hey, you don't belong here. You're not enough.' I felt like I was an impostor, and I was going to get discovered as not being enough. That feeling followed me for 15 years in my NASCAR career." He continued, "This may sound like humble bragging, but it's true. I had a career that most NASCAR fans would envy! Multiple championships, I met the Who's Who, I traveled across the nation. It was a crazy journey I was on. Having great success, but still feeling like I didn't belong. Growing up, I was an average kid. Not a great athlete. Suddenly, I'm working on a NASCAR pit crew! How did I get here? Do I really belong here?

"I had a desire to be the successful one at the top, but I didn't have the belief system in place. Subconsciously, because I didn't believe it, I was self-sabotaging myself with procrastination, failure to launch, perfection. It sounds terrible because I know that people say, 'You had an amazing career!' Yes, I did. I had multiple championships, I made a great living, I did live TV for Fox Sports, It was a dream career! But there was this undercurrent of 'I'm going to be discovered as this average high school baseball player, with small time experience, and now I'm at the big time.' It always haunted me."

Over the years, Matt Clark overcame his own fraud fears. Now, he helps organizations build winning teams, both mentally and in competition. Influenced by great business peers and his research on mindset, he's tackled impostor syndrome. In a March 2023 TEDx Talk at Babson College, he declared, "I worked hard for my success, and I deserve it… I am enough. I am a champion"

Wouldn't it be great to have an entire team of champions who think like this? You can. And you can be one of them.

Lead Like Lively

In the beginning of this book I told the embarrassing story of getting the hiccups in PSL on my first day in the control room. That wasn't the only lesson I learned that day.

Get Your Best People to Give Their Best Effort

When I first walked into that control room I was intimidated because everyone else was so much more experienced than me. The engine test we were conducting was sponsored by NATO, and there were visitors from around the world. I felt outclassed. However, I was rattled the most by one man in particular. His name was Lively Bryant, the Lead Operations Engineer for the test. He stood in the middle of the control room, like Captain Kirk commanding the Enterprise. I'd heard of him, but had not met him. He was an African American mountain of a man, about 6'3", built like a linebacker, with a stately intensity that felt fierce and imposing. I was scared of him.

As the Lead Operations Engineer, Lively oversaw everything that happened during the test. Nothing happened without his knowledge or permission. The mood in the room was due mostly to his intense demeanor, reflecting the gravity of his role. He was responsible for maintaining order to ensure that procedures are followed, data is collected accurately, and the safety of all personnel is guaranteed. After all, we had a live fighter aircraft jet engine in operation in the test cell just a few yards away.

When I made my way to the one empty chair, my goal was to not be disruptive in any, and certainly not irritate Lively.

But when the hiccups started, and all those heads snapped in my direction, every bit of dignity slid out of me. I locked eyes with Lively. I thought, "This is it! My career is over before it started!" Time stood still. I was nervous. The crew was nervous. God was nervous.

I watched him as he stood there. And then he said…nothing.

Not a thing. He just smiled and turned back to his work.

Every head in the room turned back to their work, and I suddenly felt okay. In that split second, my damaged dignity was restored. He gave me the "Good Housekeeping Seal of Approval."

John Maxwell says, "People buy into the leader before they buy into the vision." When Lively preserved my dignity, I knew I'd follow him anywhere. I bought into him as a leader before I even knew if he had a vision.

When the CEO is the CEI

Leadership is not rocket science. At its most basic, it is another word for influence. And every connection we have with another person is a chance to influence them. It's predictable, measurable and repeatable. But leadership involves people, and people can be messy. They're not predictable, measurable, or repeatable. It doesn't require a college degree or any advanced certifications. Anyone can lead because anyone can influence.

The question becomes, how do you become the leader that people want to follow? Start by believing that every interaction you have with someone is a powerful moment that endures. Your exchange with someone can change someone.

That may sound a bit ethereal, but it's true. Every decision you make was somehow influenced by another person. It may have been through a personal conversation, or something you heard, something you read, or something you observed…it may have been in the past, in the present, or in your hopeful vision of the future. Someone impacted you.

It goes both ways. Your influence, which is more than you think, is transcendental. Do you remember algebra class, learning about transcendental numbers, like pi and e? They're numbers that are unusual, unending, and without any pattern. Yet they're pervasive, useful and powerful. So is your influence.

That PSL control room incident with Lively showed me that even a casual interaction with someone can affect them for a very, very long time. It happened over forty years ago, and I still tell the story! Leadership is influence that endures. Don't underestimate the significance of even a small, shared moment with someone. You may very well be restoring their dignity after they've uttered their own "hiccup heard round the world." (By the way, I got to know Lively very well at NASA. He was a fantastic guy, well-liked and respected by the entire PSL community, including me.)

Lively did five specific things that helped.

He offered kindness: He smiled a "I've done that before!" smile that was kind. He could have commanded me to leave, but he didn't. I'm sure he knew I was embarrassed on many levels. His kindness shattered my shame.

Get Your Best People to Give Their Best Effort

He modeled right behavior: When he said nothing, everyone else followed suit. Nobody called me out on it, and everyone went right back to their work. He led by example.

He kept priorities in line: He kept the main thing the main thing. I'm sure if it was something more disruptive than hiccups that interrupted him, he'd act appropriately, but his focus was on the project goal, not an individual's shortcomings. I felt part of the larger effort, not an impediment to it.

He preserved my dignity: His kindness alleviated my embarrassment. He didn't have to say a word to do that. In fact, saying anything would have been less impactful to me.

He established trust: Knowing he had my back made me want to have his. He built a foundation of trust not just with me but with the whole crew. I admired him every day from that day forward. He was a great leader!

Your interactions with your team don't have to be grand gestures of managerial excellence. They just need to be sincere, kind, trustworthy. Impostor syndrome is a personal and difficult issue, and it could be hard for a team member to talk about it or confess it to you their manager. But if you can see every interaction as a way to build the trust bridge, your work is easier. These next chapters will give you the tactics to lead better, but overall the best strategy behind the tactics is to lead like Lively.

17

Feeding the Insecurity Monster

Now that we've unpacked how impostor syndrome looks from the outside and what might be going on in someone's head, let's shift gears and focus on the work environment. In this chapter, we'll dive into how the corporate culture might be unknowingly feeding into the insecurity "monster" exacerbating your employees' impostor syndrome. Here are some things to evaluate.

Is your environment high-pressure with unrealistic expectations or intense competition? Many industries, especially manufacturing, healthcare, retail, construction, and logistics, are filled with quotas, deadlines, production schedules, high-ticket deliverables, and safety concerns. When you add unrealistic goals, mandatory overtime, or limited time off, it can foster stress and self-doubt, even in your top performers.

One of my clients, a manager in a manufacturing company, was worried that impostor syndrome in the productivity-driven environment caused employees to hold back from speaking up

Get Your Best People to Give Their Best Effort

about issues on the production line. Suppressing confidence is one thing, but prioritizing throughput over safety and quality is dangerous and costly.

A corporate culture that fosters competition and comparison can lead to feelings of inadequacy, even among top performers. For example, "employee of the month" awards aim to recognize excellence, but can make others feel like they're falling short. Constant comparison can make top performers doubt their achievements, discouraging them from pushing harder.

In sales organizations, quotas drive performance but also create a high-pressure, competitive environment where employees feel they must constantly prove their worth. Academic pedigree checks, like, "Oh, you went to XYZ University? Interesting..." can also breed self-doubt. People question if they're valued for their skills or their diploma. When the workplace becomes a battleground of accolades and credentials, impostor syndrome can take root.

How do you offer feedback and recognition? Organizations that provide feedback that is personal, regular, specific and positive will flourish. Find the way to frame the constructive feedback so it lands well, without criticism or harshness. Don't neglect the areas that need attention, but be cautious how you address it. You may already know that it takes a ratio of three positive comments to balance one negative comment. This helps in maintaining a positive atmosphere while still addressing areas for improvement.

Even your champion performers need it. The Feb 16, 2024 episode of the podcast, *On Purpose with Jay Shetty* titled, "Three Ways to Build Inner Confidence" offers fascinating insight into understanding the relevance to impostor syndrome.

He explained a difference between *inner confidence* and *outer confidence,* which are both rooted in our need for validation.

Inner confidence is the desire to *be better.* It comes from our own internal validation based in wanting to improve oneself, not for the sake of others' approval, but for your own satisfaction and growth.

Feeding the Insecurity Monster

Outer confidence is the desire to *be seen as better* and comes from external validation, the human desire to be acknowledged and esteemed by others. It's about presenting oneself in a way that generates approval and admiration from the external world.

So, how is this related to impostor syndrome?

Suppose a person does the hard work to accomplish something big. Maybe they lost a lot of weight, or secured a big client contract, or won a competition. The work to do it was grueling! It took a combination of talent, skill, perseverance, circumstance, timing, external influences, intelligence, coaching, research, discipline, and all sorts of other factors, and they succeeded. People celebrate and congratulate them, and it feels terrific. *External validation begets external confidence,* which feels nice…for a short time.

We can get addicted to it, but it can replace and even silence the internal validation, or the practice of acknowledging to yourself your skills and successes. This internal validation is the true impetus for driving the intentional work we do to pursue self-awareness and personal growth. It's extremely empowering and sustaining. Silencing it by relying on the external validation offered by others is perilous because we lose heart and motivation.

Here's the problem: as time passes, the external validation offered by others eventually goes silent because the victory was either so far in the rear-view mirror, or the ongoing success behavior has become so part of your identity, that you're just seen as competent. Nobody praises a teenager for the act of walking, even though at age one it was cause for celebration. Even if it takes a lot of work to do that same thing, to maintain or repeat the success, nobody really knows how hard it is to do it other than you, the person who did it.

In the absence of external validation, the internal self-talk goes wonky and defaults to a negative script. "I must not be that special! I've lost my touch! I'm not qualified!" It's no news flash to know that negative self-talk creates a negative self-image. Internal confidence takes a massive hit.

Get Your Best People to Give Their Best Effort

Everyone needs to work on finding their own internal validation. By recognizing their own strengths and achievements, they can make real progress in overcoming impostor syndrome and step into their power with confidence. But leaders must play a role. Commit to celebrate your team's victories, acknowledge their growth, and give them chances to develop new skills. Help them help themselves.

How do you address isolation, communication and clarity? This was covered in the earlier chapter about COVID, but there's an element of the physical office/organization environment that should not be overlooked or overstated. Isolation.

As I mentioned previously, my earliest task at NASA included working with an analog computer to solve a problem called "engine stall." An analog computer, even in the early '80s, was a dinosaur machine. Picture a big telephone switchboard with wires crisscrossing all over, plugged into holes, controlled by dials and knobs. I had never seen one before, not even in college, so I had to learn how to use it. It was located in the computer building, called the Research Analysis Center, or the RAC building. This was years before PCs, and all computing power was centralized at the RAC. The analog computer was so archaic; it was in a small back corner of the building, in a restricted and locked area. I worked there eight hours a day, with four other young male engineers, who had a few more years' experience than I did. Our boss was in a different building, clear across the NASA complex. I felt isolated, clueless, and without any courage to ask for help when I needed it. It all added up to me feeling like an incompetent loser, filled with shamed. I didn't last long in that project before I requested a transfer to the PSL test facility.

Had I stayed in that RAC building, I would have withered. Not only did the isolation not match my personality, but it was also the worst place to put a brand new engineer. Out of sight, out of mind, out of touch, out of joy.

Clarity is another factor related to isolation and communication. If a person isn't given clear goals, with clear expectations in a clear manner, that fosters uncertainty. Word of

Feeding the Insecurity Monster

mouth communication, unwritten rules, "that's the way we've always done things" are part of every organization, but they do more harm than good. In my early days at NASA, long before I was a manger, I attended a status meeting in the main administration building, in the large fancy conference room. (Well, it was fancy for NASA. It had carpet, something most buildings lacked.) There was a huge conference table that accommodated about twenty people, with more chairs along the room's perimeter. I walked in and took a seat at the table. People along the wall stared at me in disbelief. I later learned that the unwritten rule was that the table was reserved for managers. I had no idea. I was so embarrassed. Something that simple set me up to always question if I was doing the right thing.

How's the mentoring and coaching? Mentoring can really help with impostor syndrome, giving people the support and validation they need. But let's be honest: most mentoring programs aren't great. They often seem like lip service, lacking real impact. They're not measured, don't feel natural, and aren't well-structured. Leaders need to step up and make mentoring more than a checkbox. This means creating programs that have clear goals, connect people based on shared interests, and check how things are going. When done right, mentoring can truly boost confidence and help tackle impostor syndrome.

Mentoring is not just for new employees. Since impostor syndrome screams the loudest in times of transition, it's beneficial to provide mentoring for people who are taking on new roles, new projects, or learning new skills/content. Having an effective mentor can assist in developing confidence and expanding influence.

Mentoring is not coaching. They overlap, but there are differences. A mentor is from within the organization or industry, and their purpose is to draw on their personal experience and expertise to guide and support. It's a longer-term relationship, focused on navigating organizational culture. Coaching is more specific and short-term, targeted at a particular skill or clear goal. The coach may or may not be part of the same organization or industry.

Get Your Best People to Give Their Best Effort

A mentor relationship is more informal than a coaching relationship. A mentor acts as a trusted advisor, where a coach acts more as a facilitator of change. Mentoring can start more organically, born out of the mentee's desire to emulate someone they admire or respect. An organization that "assigns" a mentor may have the right desire, but could be missing the mark. With an assigned mentor, the relationship can feel more forced, sometimes tangled in office politics. On the other hand, mentoring relationships that form naturally feel more genuine and flexible, aligning better with your personal goals and needs.

The structure of mentoring can be more relaxed, conversational where the mentor shares stories and observations from their experience. Coaches use more tools and methodologies like active listening, feedback, SMART goal setting, and accountability.

Because impostor syndrome is so intimate and personal, both mentoring and coaching provide value. Mentoring from within the organization can guide people through their change of responsibility or role. The mentee can get valuable insights on things like the politics, people, process, and priorities they'll need to know to do their new job. Getting real-life insights from someone "who's been there, done that" is so valuable in mitigating the fear of stepping into a new role.

Coaching someone through impostor syndrome is also critical, but should be provided by someone with specific knowledge of impostor syndrome. It's a nuanced and complex experience. The Impostor Syndrome Institute, co-founded by Valerie Young and Carolyn Herfurth, is the world's leading resource of impostor syndrome solutions. They offer impostor syndrome-informed training to coaches who want to add this element to their toolbox. I highly recommend finding a coach with this training. (PS: I can help.) However, you can provide coaching guidance to your team even if you're not a certified coach. I cover that in Appendix B.

What are your organizational values? Despite what the organizational mission and vision is, values are communicated by everyday conversations and actions. Corporate websites have

Feeding the Insecurity Monster

grand (and often vague) statements like, "We act with integrity and honesty in all we do." Or "We lead by example and inspire others to achieve their best." But what is the real deal? What are employees seeing at ground level, in day-to-day interactions with their boss, coworkers, vendors and clients? Here are some questions to ask yourself about your organizational culture.

- Which is more important, creativity or hard work? Why?
- Which is more important, the product or the process?
- As a leader, am I more committed to *my* success than the success and growth of my team?
- Have we set unrealistic standards that promote perfectionism or unreachable goals?
- Are we recognizing the effort and outcome of everyone?
- Do we have a good balance of individualism and teamwork? Or are we too focused on one over the other?
- Do we have a good balance between competition and collaboration?
- How do we *really* view failure?
- Do we value curiosity and innovation, while also valuing consistency, legacy and stability?
- Do we *really* walk the talk of our mission, vision and value statements?
- Do we preserve everyone's dignity? Or do we unknowingly suppress it and demand conformity?
- How do we discipline those who do wrong?
- How do we handle dissension and difficult employees?
- Do I model the behavior I want from my team?
- Am I aware of the systemic or circumstantial influences on impostor syndrome? (Refer back to chapter 7, "You Mean I'm Normal?")

Give these some serious thought if you want to make serious progress in leading your team

18

Make Friends Who Make Memories

About fifteen years after I left NASA, I was at a wedding where I ran into Jeff, a former NASA coworker. Like me, Jeff served as the facility manager of one of the large test research facilities. Unlike me, he remained at NASA, and moved into an upper-management position.

I gave him a huge hug, squealing. "Jeff! It's so good to see you! How are things going at NASA?"

"It's pretty good." Then he gave a high-level summary of what he's doing and where he fits in the agency's structure.

"So, tell me," I asked, "Who is still around that I would remember?" He shook his head. "I don't think there's anybody left that you would remember." He sounded wistful.

I could almost read his mind. During our time together at NASA, our group of facility managers forged a super-glued bond. There were eight of us, and we had a blast together. As we wrestled the rapids of our tough jobs, we managed to laugh and support each other, while building great friendships. Our Monday staff meetings were a highlight for me, because it was the one place where we could let our frustrations out, beyond the eyes and ears of the rest of the office, and stand with each other in

Get Your Best People to Give Their Best Effort

good and hard times. Even after fifteen years, that alliance brought on a sweet, sentimental nostalgia.

That camaraderie was due to our boss, John Schaefer. He was the best boss I ever had. He was brilliant, hardworking, insightful, tough, hilarious, kind, and visionary. He was fierce in his support of his facility managers, advocating and defending us. But he also piled the work on us. He often said, "I'm going to give you work until your eyes roll." And he did. But we did the work, because we respected him and had a rabid loyalty to him.

Now, lest you think this is getting too touchy-feely, it's not. The connections you forge in your team can be powerful and long-lasting. John was a master at fostering a team camaraderie with his affable personality and respectful management style. He didn't know it, but he was addressing one of the deepest capacities of human beings: the need to connect. People long to connect to other people, to a group identity, and to a greater vision or cause. Connecting leads to flourishing.

No doubt, our group chemistry inspired to get a ridiculous amount of work done. We were each other's cheering squad, sounding board, and feedback factory. For me, I know it was a safe place for the times I felt the sting of self-doubt. My connections to my teammates alleviated it.

John was intentional with creating this camaraderie. Some of the things he did were:

- He wanted a team whose individual personalities meshed well. He was transparent about it when he promoted me, saying, "You fit well."
- We had regular outings, like Friday lunch at Southpark Mall or Elsa's Mexican restaurant. One evening, we all went to a dinner theater with our significant others, creating a great memory.
- His weekly staff meetings were the lifeblood of our operation. We all had the opportunity to speak our minds, with no judgment or criticism from him.
- He inspired us to be as autonomous as possible. If we had a facility problem, he's say, "Not my circus. Not my

Make Friends Who Make Memories

monkey." But if we needed him to use his authority to do something we couldn't, he would do it in a heartbeat.
- We had one-on-ones with him anytime we needed. That was especially valuable when I was first promoted.
- He was a great communicator, especially with information from above. NASA, like any other business was wrought with politics, conflicts and split loyalties. Budget cuts, manpower issues and scheduling problems were always hard. He was a reliable source of new information and potential changes coming down the pike.
- He was jovial and fun, but serious and authoritative when needed. He corrected us with kindness, never diminishing our dignity. His "walk the halls" management style kept him aware and available without being a micromanager
- He protected and elevated our status with perks and privileges, like having two-person offices instead of the normal 3–4 person spaces, which made us feel special and fostered loyalty. John was a master at delegating and asking for updates, making me feel important to the team.

Our group was so tight, that even after I left NASA, we'd meet every year for a Christmas lunch. At one of these lunches, I was entertaining them with stories of my new focus as a professional speaker on the topic of impostor syndrome. They all nodded and said, "Oh, yeah, I felt that too." I said to John, "You were the best boss I ever had. You were smart and really good, but you had a knack for pulling us together as a strong team." He paused and smiled. "Well, thank you for that. The truth is, I didn't always know what I was doing."

Whoa. Even the greatest leaders can feel impostor syndrome. But they don't let it derail their work at leading extraordinary teams. It starts with being relational and cultivating rabid and robust camaraderie. Sometimes it can happen naturally, but if you're intentional, it's worth the work.

Get Your Best People to Give Their Best Effort

19

Set Up for Failure?

When building good teams, you surely intend them to succeed. Building relationships certainly helps, but are you doing what you can to insure that success? Or are you setting them up for failure?

One gray, rainy morning I was driving on a busy two-lane road. About a block ahead, I saw a utility truck blocking the other lane; in my lane I saw headlights of oncoming traffic as cars from that blocked lane maneuvered around the truck. As I approached the truck, I stopped to let those cars make their way around the truck and back into their lane.

I suddenly noticed a utility worker standing off to the right of my lane, about two car lengths ahead of me, holding one of those portable reversible "STOP/SLOW" signs. He was frantically waving the "STOP" side of the sign at me. Apparently I didn't stop in the right place for him, and he was mad. Or maybe just terrified that I'd roll right through and cause an accident.

He was standing in a bad spot. He wasn't far enough upstream of the utility truck to stop me sooner. But in the rainy weather, I had my eyes on the oncoming headlights, not him. He was responsible to control the traffic, yet he was not in the right place to do it. I felt bad for him, and I thought I would offer some help.

Get Your Best People to Give Their Best Effort

He switched his sign to "slow," and I started to move. As I got to him, I stopped and rolled down my passenger window. I said, "I'm sorry I didn't see you sooner. You might want to stand a little further upstream because I didn't even see you until I was nearly on top of you."

Irritation prickled his voice. "We had a sign back there at the intersection." (The intersection was a good quarter mile back.)

"Oh, I didn't see any signs."

"Didn't you see the truck?" he asked.

"Yes, I did, and I saw headlights coming at me, but I didn't see you or the signs."

He pointed to his fluorescent orange vest. "How could you miss me?" He was astonished and frustrated.

Oops. In the rainy dreary gray weather, it was the first I even noticed the bright vest. I said, "No, I didn't see you. I was looking at headlights." I paused. "I think it would be a good idea to have two of you, in between the lanes, one close, and one a little further away from the truck, so people can see you better."

He looked at me with contempt, and sneered "I'm the only one here!"

"I know. I'm just making a suggestion. That's all." I said. I rolled up my window and got moving.

He was set up for failure in four ways. First, the job really required more than one person. Second, he didn't have the resources to fix the problem. Third, his grumpy personality was not a good fit for a position dealing with an irritated and irritating public. And fourth, he didn't want to fix the problem, even with someone's help. (Remember the fixed/growth mindset chapter? I think I met a fixed mindset person!)

I'm sure he was a decent hard-working guy. But he was not equipped for the job he was to do. I wonder if he went back to his boss at lunch and complained about the lady who stopped traffic to offer her opinion on his work.

As a leader, you know that mitigating failure includes the basics like assessing the job and its requirements, matching the right person to the right job, and developing contingency plans to think through the obstacles. But when impostor syndrome is part of the equation, the job becomes more nuanced. You may be setting up team members for failure, and exacerbating their impostor syndrome experience. Here are some questions to consider.

Are you providing them the necessary resources? When the right resources are scarce, the pressure to perform with limited tools or support can heighten feelings of inadequacy. People might feel that they should be able to succeed despite these limitations, which can lead to self-doubt when they struggle. Without proper support from the right people, team members can feel isolated in the roles, and believe they're the only ones struggling. Your role? Secure the resources however you can. Get them yourself. Advocate on behalf of your team. Reallocate responsibilities. Reassess deadlines and goals. Be transparent about limitations and see how the team can work within or around them.

Do you notice if they won't ask for help? This could be a sign of fear of having inadequacies exposed. In addition, when help is not available, it can reinforce belief that one should manage to do it alone. This may work well, right up to the moment it doesn't due to added complexity, unforeseen problem, or something taking longer than expected. That leads to feelings of incompetence and not deserving the position. To address this, be upfront and open about your observations. John, my NASA boss had to do this with me. He said, "You know, you don't have to do it all yourself. You have an entire crew and engineering staff to help. And they're good at their job. Ask for their help!" Then he brainstormed some ideas with me to help me cultivate a more cooperative team-spirit.

Are you certain you've matched skills to the job? This was covered in a previous chapter about the skill gap. More important is the *character* gap. If you need a role filled by a person with qualities like curiosity, professionalism, or optimism, make sure you get that right person in the right job. It's also good to ask them, "Do you like your work?" On the positive side, it shows you're concerned and will cement your awareness of whether your team members are engaged and enjoying their work. By

Get Your Best People to Give Their Best Effort

fostering open communication you'll get hints about their impostor syndrome feelings, while creating a trusting environment where they are okay with honest sharing. However, the downside is that if not handled carefully, it might make them worry about potential repercussions. They might fear that admitting they don't enjoy their work could reflect poorly on them or affect their job security. To avoid these pitfalls, it's important to ask the question within a supportive and non-threatening context, ensuring they know their feedback won't be used against them.

Seeing how leaders can accidentally set their team up for failure is helpful to prevent this in the future. However, it's not to say that all failure should be avoided. Sometimes teams need to face a failure to create success.

20

Let Them Fail

Even rocket scientists must deal with failure. Adam Steltzner, the renowned NASA JPL (Jet Propulsion Lab) engineer and team leader is best known for his pivotal technical and leadership roles in the exploration of Saturn (Cassini), Jupiter (Galileo), and Mars (Pathfinder and Mars Exploration Rovers, (MER)). In his book *The Right Kind of Crazy*, he details the long and arduous journey of overcoming what seemed impossible: landing the Curiosity rover craft on the surface of Mars.

The book is a fascinating tale of courageous curiosity (pun intended) intertwined with (and sometimes strangled by) the layers of government complexities. In the book, he tells a story of one of the predecessor programs to Curiosity, the Mars Climate Orbiter, a vehicle that was to explore the atmosphere around Mars without landing on the surface. The vehicle was launched in December, 1998, but eight months later, in September 1999, as it approached Mars atmosphere, NASA permanently lost contact with it. Investigations later concluded that due to a mix-up between metric and English measurement units, design calculations were wrong, and the craft got too close to the planet, which caused it to burn up in the atmosphere. While Steltzner

Get Your Best People to Give Their Best Effort

was not involved in this orbiter program, reviewing it taught him a lot about leadership, problem-solving, team building, innovation, and questioning the status quo. He also developed an appetite for asking tough questions, involving himself in spirited technical discussions, and getting comfortable with uncertainty and doubt. In his book he says, "I used to think of leadership as a sign of power. At JPL I learned it is also a sign of service. You are gifting your thinking of how the group should attack a problem."

This was during NASA's era of doing business "Faster, Better, Cheaper (FBC)," a time I remember well. A bit of back story: In the early '90s the NASA administrator, Dan Goldin, implemented the FBC policies. It was in response to severe cuts in congressional funding, coupled with escalating technology complexities which caused longer development timelines and massive schedule overruns, especially in large programs. It was in stark contrast to what had become a normal operating mindset at the agency for decades. In 1961, when President Kennedy announced his plan to "land a man on the moon and safely return him to earth before the end of the decade," that crystallized the agency's focus on a goal. Do it fast, do it right, no matter the cost. Turns out, it cost a lot. But it was a huge win for the country, so celebration prevailed over budget concerns, and NASA thrived. Over time, NASA's culture became one which valued speed and technical success over fiscal concerns. FBC changed that, and financial responsibility became as important.

It sounds great in theory. In practice, it became clear that if you have a "Faster, Better, Cheaper" focus, the best you can do is pick two of the three. By the time MER was in progress in 2000, FBC dictated many smart cost-cutting, quick turnaround efforts that made sense. Things like having the rovers share parts, implementing parallel construction schedules, and using off-the-shelf designs dating back to the 1970s Viking missions saved money and shortened schedules. But there were also cuts in manpower, leaving not enough people to check all the data…including whether numbers were in inches or centimeters, kilograms or pounds. It was a costly management decision leading to an oversight and costly accident. The Mars Climate Orbiter program cost $327.6M, and the craft was a total loss.

Losing an entire rover craft in the atmosphere of another planet is an epic fail. I already described my own much smaller loss of equipment when I melted the infra-red camera in PSL. Yet the way you bounce back from the loss, whether huge or small is the same. There's always a trade-off between progress and the risk of failure. It's either a big flop or a jubilant success. How will you respond in a way that shows your team strong leadership?

Regardless of the outcome, this is true: people always deserve to have their dignity preserved. It's highly unlikely that it was bad intentions that caused the failure. Attacking people's character isn't the thing to do. Pointing out flaws in their decision should be a learning opportunity, not a shaming one. Great leaders understand that taking risks runs the risk of failure. Steltzner was known for his bold and innovative leadership and problem-solving style, which lead him to push hard for an unconventional approach to landing Curiosity on Mars. Some thought his approach was kooky, but it ended up working. He saw setbacks as opportunities to learn and grow and push the boundaries of technology, while encouraging his team to not wallow in failure. He is quoted as saying "Great works and great follies may be indistinguishable at the outset." In his book he writes, "I came to realize in building spacecraft as in most other complex endeavors, success or failure depends on those human factors…the quality of interaction and the clarity of communication…every bit as much as it does on the technology."

In many cases, you won't have such intense pressure on you. Lives are not at stake. The stability of the free world is not in the balance. You probably won't lose a vehicle that cost $327.6M. But failure is part of life, and a part of progress. Leaving room for failure, or rather the proper response to failure is essential.

Failure isn't the villain in our success stories; it's a key player. Great leaders know that preventing every failure isn't realistic or even helpful. Instead, they create spaces where it's okay to make mistakes, learn from them, and bounce back stronger. This

Get Your Best People to Give Their Best Effort

approach is important when dealing with impostor syndrome, where fear of failure can be paralyzing. When you can learn to separate the mistake from the mistake-maker, you'll be well on your way to learning a pivotal aspect of leading people who struggle with impostor syndrome and are committed to perfection or more wary of feedback. By encouraging a culture where failure is seen as a stepping stone, leaders can help their teams build confidence and resilience.

Sixty Percent?

My keynote closing story is about a woman named Denali Lumma, an IT consultant with an impressive history working for companies like Salesforce, Walmart, and Uber. As a child, she was labeled as gifted because good grades came easy. This caused her to equate her worth with the outcome, not the effort. She stuck to this low-effort approach which worked just fine for her. At least, until it didn't. Like any child, she tried something hard, and when it failed she said, "OUCH! I don't like that. I'm going to stick to what's easy and avoid what's hard. Who cares if people think I'm lazy. I'd rather be seen as lazy than stupid."

She adopted this 60 percent effort approach all the way through college. She got good grades, graduated with a computer science degree, and stepped into her first IT job. Like many women in STEM, she was surrounded by mostly men, but they championed her and buoyed her, and created opportunities for her to flourish.

After a few years, she started to feel an internal tension. She looked at her career and thought, "Hmmm. I give it 60 percent effort, and I have a lot of help doing it. I guess I'm not only lazy, I really am stupid." Ouch.

In 2010 she'd had enough of playing small. She decided to try an experiment. She said to herself, "What would happen if I took on a project that was way beyond my skills, doomed to fail? What would happen if I threw myself into it 100 percent? I've never done that before."

Let Them Fail

That's a powerful question for both you and your teams. "What would happen if...?" It demonstrates courageous curiosity that will most certainly lead to discomfort and uncertainty, but also tremendous transformation. It can lead to an internal journey of self-discovery and boldness. Asking hard questions and doing hard things leads to making huge progress.

Denali took on this tough software development project. It was like a cancerous growth, causing the company to lose money, anger customers, and sacrifice market share. It tentacled into all areas of the company: development, testing, marketing, customer service, legal. But she took it on, and committed to throwing herself into it 100 percent.

She gathered a team, laid out plans, visualized success, and they got to work. They worked long hours, day after day for weeks. There were fiery meetings, confusing questions, technical roadblocks. They toiled through status updates, software reviews, legal issues, marketing problems, development concerns. She worked harder than she ever had. She thought, "If this project fails, it won't be because I didn't try!"

The effort paid off. Within record time, they had a working prototype. Alpha and beta testing followed soon after, exceeding all expectations. They set a rollout date to release the software to the general population. Everyone was jubilant!

Except Denali. She had serious reservations. She said, "There are some flaws in the software. It has bugs. It doesn't scale well. I don't think it ready yet. I must choose what to do, and I only see two choices."

Can you imagine how she felt? She's worked hard for a dream, and her worst fear is right in front of her. Two choices. On one hand, if she releases flawed software, her boss is mad, her customers are furious, and her team is embarrassed. On the other hand, if she cancelled the rollout, her boss is mad, her customers are furious, and her team is embarrassed. It's lose-lose.

Facing the impostor syndrome *will* feel like a battle. It will be scary. Disruptive. Paralyzing. Even lose-lose.

Persevere anyway. Push through it anyway. Because on the other side of the push is transformation. Like Stelzner said,

Get Your Best People to Give Their Best Effort

"Great works and great follies may be indistinguishable at the outset." The same can be said for transformation and destruction.

What did Denali do? At the last minute, she canceled the rollout. To the outsider, it looked like a massive failure. Denali said, "It was humiliating, and not without serious consequences. But internally, I was proud of what I had done. For the first time in my life, I did the hard work."

For her, the process of leading the team was rich and rewarding. The power of the defeat was diffused by the awareness of her influence and untapped strengths. And it got better. The pause in the release allowed the team to work longer to fine-tune the software and they released a far superior product that took the market by storm and led the company to unprecedented levels of prestige. Her team was regarded as experts, she was asked by other companies to solve similar problems, allowing her to monetize the solution. She said, "That failure catapulted me to success faster and further than I ever imagined."

You are not the failure. Rather, what you did, failed.

Failure can be both humiliating and empowering. Impostor syndrome often steals that empowering opportunity due to a limited vision of what success *should be*. Sometimes success follows failure, but it looks different than what you expected. Sometimes the only path to success is through failure. Those who face scary situations can find themselves energized. Failure may cause terror and humiliation, but it's survivable and even thriveable. Like gold purified in a flame, greatness is forged through enduring failures.

Everyone has intrinsic value, even if they fail. Instead of saying, "I'm an idiot. I'm the mistake," it's better to say, "I made a mistake. I'm human." Striving to avoid all mistakes is impossible and counterproductive. Authentic people allow themselves to fail, understanding that falling is necessary to rise up.

Let Them Fail

For those with impostor syndrome, changing this thought process is like swimming upstream. It takes diligent focus and a will of steel to replace negative thoughts with objective facts. It's not easy. Impostors live in fear, and falling short feels like death. Repeating and embracing the facts of their skills and circumstances, even in failure, is crucial. Failure doesn't mean you are a failure; it just means that something else happened. If a terrific baseball batter comes to bat and crushes the ball, hitting it to the wall, he did a fantastic job. But if the right fielder runs and makes a diving lunge and catches the ball, he did a fantastic job too. Nobody failed. It's just that sometimes there's no room for simultaneous successes.

Let's dive into why it's important to know what your team members love to do and how tapping into their core motivation can boost morale and make the team more successful and innovative.

21

Fueled Up!

Have you ever been so immersed in a task that you lost track of time? Psychologist Mihaly Csikszentmihalyi calls this state "flow." It is the optimal state of consciousness where individuals feel and perform their best. People experiencing flow report increased productivity, creativity, and happiness for up to three days. Flow occurs when a person's skills are matched well to the challenge. There's no anxiety due to difficulty, or boredom due to simplicity. It's as if the process itself is a fuel source to charge someone up.

For leaders, knowing what triggers this flow state, i.e., what the right fuel is for each team member, will optimize performance and maximize outcome. Identifying the "fuel source" of each team member helps them find joy in their work, recognize their unique capabilities, and operate at peak performance. Just as different aircraft or vehicles require different fuel, individuals need the right fuel to perform their best. Understanding each team member's personal fuel source also helps combat impostor syndrome, freeing them from the pressure to be fired up by what doesn't fuel them up.

There are five different fuel types common to every person. At our core, each of us wants to Connect, Cultivate, Continue, Conquer, and/or Craft. They are different from personality styles identified by profile tests such as Myers–Briggs or DISC. Personality is the way we enter the world. The fuel sources describe what we extract from the world, to enter into the world. It's the energy we require, the fuel that lights us up. I'm going to do a very brief overview of the fuel sources, but for more depth, go to this link for the bonus content: https://maureenz.com/GYBPbonus

The five fuel types are:

Connectors

These socializers like bringing people together, making new connections and building community. Being a connector is more about *how* you connect with people, not *how many* people you know. But their winsome personality may have the darker side of impostor syndrome, cloaked as "the Fascinator." (Refer to Chapter 2.)

Cultivators

They coach, train and mentor. They also organize, plan, and support. They will establish order and refinement in a process and an environment. They like the process more than the product, so tie their recognition to their effort, not the result.

Continuers

They love consistency, predictability, and history. My dear friend and fellow professional speaker, Jack Park, with whom I coauthored a book about The Ohio State University football program, is a walking, talking encyclopedia of OSU football history. He is a textbook Continuer.

Continuers may be hesitant to initiate change that could rock the boat. As a leader you can affirm there is no judgment or recourse for speaking up, even if it's disruptive. Continuers need to see that their voice is necessary to the bigger picture. Knowing they can leave a legacy could embolden them to speak up with the assurance that they matter.

Conquerors

These people strive to win, overcome, circumvent, control, or outwit something or someone. If they want to take charge, break a bad habit, meet a deadline, or clean out a closet, that's conquering.

When a conqueror with impostor syndrome receives an award or is recognized for an achievement, he could still have self-doubt that poisons the achievement because he is thinking of the ways he could have done better. He may also be torn because he has a strong desire to overcome or be in charge, yet he has enough fear that keeps him a bit timid. These conquerors may instead find other outlets outside of work from which to draw their conquering fuel.

Crafters

Crafters build, construct, assemble, and improvise. They are creative, innovative, and independent. They often like working with their hands (for example, builders, artists, and craftspeople) and often contribute brilliant ideas in brainstorming sessions. They may produce something physical, or they produce something logistical or organizational, such as a different way to do things, or a new organizational structure.

There are overlaps between these five fuel sources. Crafters and conquerors both use their perspective to tackle a problem. Continuers and connectors are often very people-oriented. Cultivators can be like crafters in their innovative approaches.

Your team members will likely have one dominant fuel source. Take the time to observe and learn where their energy originates, and then take steps to foster them to flourish.

Connect the Dots

When you know what fuels your team members up, you can start to see how these passions align with their unique skills and strengths. This is the key because it helps them see their own abilities in a new light. By recognizing and celebrating these unique skills, we can eliminate the dreaded compare and despair trap that often creeps up in team settings. It leads to feelings of inadequacy, envy and overwhelm, as well as shame

Get Your Best People to Give Their Best Effort

discouragement and despair. It's a mess. This is where we start to "Connect the Dots."

What's that? Glad you asked.

In my keynote, I guide the audience through an exercise that is the most remembered and repeated part of the presentation. It's hard to understand fully without experiencing it in person, but I described a version of it in my first book on impostor syndrome, *Pushing Your Envelope: How Smart People Defeat Self-Doubt and Live with Bold Enthusiasm.* For your enjoyment, you can download both that chapter and a video clip from my keynote so you can get a feel for the exercise. Find them here:

https://maureenz.com/GYBPbonus

In the exercise, I introduce the value of personal and professional expertise using a metaphor of a circle that I call your DOT. It's an invisible circle that includes all your expertise and experience. People with impostor syndrome feel inadequate when comparing their DOT to someone else's DOT. This distorted perception often leads to the "compare and despair" cycle, where you imagine others see a larger DOT in you than you see in yourself, and you perceive someone else's DOT as even more impressive.

The reality, however, is far more optimistic. Everyone has their own unique DOT, and no two are the same. Even if everyone's DOT is laid side-by-side, together they wouldn't equal the sum of all knowledge in existence. This perspective helps alleviate the pressure to know everything, which is both impossible and unhealthy.

Overcoming "DOT envy" is crucial. Even brilliant minds like Einstein struggled with self-doubt. Wanting to "switch your DOT" with others, (i.e. wanting their skill or expertise or reputation) is unproductive; instead, recognize your expertise within your circle of influence. Your DOT includes not just skills and abilities, but also character traits like creativity, work ethic, and persistence. These traits, which are constant throughout life, form the foundation of how you face adversity and contribute to your success. The next chapter goes into more details on character traits.

Fueled Up!

The key takeaway is that your combination of knowledge, skills, and character traits makes you valuable in your own right. When you focus on your own DOT and its inherent worth, you can combat impostor syndrome, approaching your professional life with more confidence and self-assurance.

22

Character Matters

A fellow speaker friend was hired to deliver a keynote for an association's annual conference. He worried about not knowing their industry, so he did extensive research, incorporating industry buzzwords, statistics, and interviews with executives and employees. He even arrived a day early to gather stories and comments from members.

The result: He nailed it. The client and audience loved it.

At first glance, this might seem like over-preparation due to impostor syndrome. However, I know this speaker is dedicated to improving his skills and serving his clients. Customizing content is a mark of professionalism in the keynote world. What seemed like an effort driven by panic actually 1 made him more successful.

Decades later, he still researches his clients to serve them better. (I do the same now; he taught me well.) It's driven by a strong work ethic, dedication, diligence, and resourcefulness, not fear of being exposed. This approach continues to make him (and me) successful.

It's difficult to distinguish between someone driven by impostor syndrome and someone motivated by positive traits. People with impostor syndrome are driven by fear, seek external validation, and fear criticism. In contrast, those with a good work

Get Your Best People to Give Their Best Effort

ethic and growth mindset strive for excellence out of genuine desire, take pride in their work, and enjoy internal satisfaction. They have a balanced view of their abilities, acknowledge areas for improvement without self-condemnation, and are open to collaboration, finding it liberating and enjoyable.

However, it's easy to let fraud fears cloud your awareness of your own character traits, causing you to undervalue, overlook, or discount them.

Here's the paradox: The character traits that you undervalue are the very traits that make you the success you are. In fact, if you struggle with impostor syndrome, it's an indication of your success. You're not successful because you have impostor syndrome. Impostor syndrome shows up as you achieve success.

People who struggle with impostor syndrome seek excellence over mediocrity. But make no mistake: the pursuit of excellence is a noble effort and a preferred one in the professional world. Continued and sustainable success is caused by great character traits, not chronic impostor syndrome.

What are your character traits? What are the traits in your team members? They can be powerful assets in navigating transitions and learning new skills. Resilience helps you bounce back from setbacks and keep moving forward, while adaptability allows you to embrace change and find creative solutions to problems. Empathy fosters strong relationships and effective collaboration, making it easier to work with others and gain support. Determination drives you to persevere through difficulties and stay committed to your goals. By recognizing and leaning on these character traits, people with impostor syndrome can build the confidence to grow and thrive, even when self-doubt tries to hold you back. These traits not only support your personal and professional development but also highlight your unique value beyond just technical skills.

The same goes for your team.

Here are three strategies to emphasize character traits for yourself and your team. Start with yourself, and then extend them to your team:

Identify your character traits. You can't value what you don't identify. Recognize your specific traits to see how they've contributed to your success. Traits are constant, so what helped you achieve present success will aid future success. Ask those who know you well, search online for tools, or use the assessment that I use in my workshops, found in Appendix A. You'll be glad you did, as the discoveries might surprise you.

Evaluate how your traits got you where you are. Choose a trait and recall situations where you used it and how it contributed to your success. If creativity is your trait, how did it help you specifically? For example my affable and energetic personality helped me get promoted to the customer-facing Facility Manager position at NASA.

Honor your own character traits. Look at the people you admire—they are often valued not just for their skills, but their character traits. Forbes magazine identified the top ten character traits of highly respected people. The list included things like humility, integrity, and compassion. Those are magnetic qualities. Don't undervalue them!

Lipstick Lessons

Years ago, I was a Sales Consultant with Mary Kay Cosmetics. It's structured as a dual-ladder direct sales company where consultants earned income through the two avenues of product sales and team building. The company provided excellent training for both aspects.

One powerful training workshop on recruiting still stands out. Typical recruiting efforts centered on telling a potential team member what the job tasks were: find customers, demonstrate makeup application, sell products, order inventory, call customers to check in, keep records, host events. Most Mary Kay recruits came from a non-selling, non-makeup background, so this was overwhelming to them. This training took a different perspective. The trainer, an engineer, evaluated common objections she received, which often centered on a lack of sales experience or makeup artistry skills.

Get Your Best People to Give Their Best Effort

She shifted her approach and started describing the qualities of successful Mary Kay consultants. Rather than focusing on the job itself, she highlighted the characteristics of individuals who excelled in this role. She emphasized traits like effective time management, eagerness to learn, a knack for multitasking, creativity, friendliness, optimism, a strong sense of family, a value for relationships, the pursuit of dreams and goals, overcoming challenges, self-care, and a desire to help others. This shift in perspective was a game changer that led to greater recruiting success by focusing on the person in the job, not just the job itself.

Why? It's because most people cannot see themselves *doing* an unfamiliar job, but they can see themselves *being* the same person in that job.

They can see their character qualities more accurately than their skills and abilities. In addition, the truth is that success in a role is more often attributed to intangible character qualities than hard skills. Hard skills can be learned. Character qualities are developed over a lifetime. In fact, hard skills are learned *because* of character qualities. Diligence, curiosity, a teachable openness…these are all the qualities that allow a person to learn a new skill.

For people who struggle with impostor syndrome, this is huge. Far too often, too much emphasis is on a lack of skills instead of identifying character traits. When faced with a new challenge (a new job, a promotion opportunity, a new project) they think, "I don't think I have what it takes to do that job. Everyone will see me as a fraud." So, they pull back, and let a wonderful opportunity go by.

When facing a time of transition (which is when impostor syndrome screams the loudest!) instead of saying "I don't have the background to do that," say, "I have the qualities that allow me to figure it out and learn something new." The personal attributes and traits that contribute to past success, such as resilience, determination, adaptability, and a growth mindset play a crucial role in the ability to navigate challenges and learn from experiences. In her book *Presence*, author Amy Cuddy defines "personal power" as "access to and control of limitless inner resources, such as our skills and abilities, our deeply held values, our true personalities, our boldest selves…it makes us more open, optimistic and risk-tolerant, therefore more likely to notice and take advantage of opportunities."

Never underestimate the power of your character traits that define the type of person you are. What you *are* determines what you *do*. The same goes for your team. Communicate that to them!

23

Flip the Scripts

Beating back the impostor syndrome requires rethinking your thoughts. There's no way around it. Accepting the negative thoughts at face-value is so destructive, but transforming them is game changing. Turning your doubts into strengths and challenges into chances to grow will be your true superpower.

You and your team will face challenges that will trigger certain thoughts. In most cases, the thought are not only negative, they're automatic. The secret is in recognizing those thoughts, and flipping the script to be positive, optimistic, and resilient, ready to tackle anything. Using positive words, even when things aren't going great, can change how people feel and react. It helps everyone focus on finding solutions and seeing the silver lining. It makes it easier to stay motivated and tackle challenges head-on. When you frame setbacks in a more upbeat way, you can keep the team energized and ready to turn problems into opportunities.

I mentioned earlier in this book that during COVID, I worked for two years at a La-Z-Boy store selling furniture and decorating homes. Every week, we'd get a status email from Chuck Hausfeld, the Vice President of Retail at the headquarters

Get Your Best People to Give Their Best Effort

location. I've never met Chuck in person, but wow…I wanted to. His emails were filled with upbeat celebratory declarations. During COVID when the worldwide supply chain was disrupted, La-Z-Boy had massive issues getting electronic components, leather and foam from suppliers, not to mention a big shortage of qualified manpower in the assembly lines and customer service. It was a difficult time. We didn't go a day at the store without a customer on the phone or in the showroom upset about something. A delay. A flaw. A fee. Before COVID, customers could get custom upholstery pieces delivered in 4–6 weeks. At the peak of COVID disruption, custom orders were taking five, six, or seven months, with leather taking up to a year. It was crazy, and customers were understandably furious. Our store staff was demoralized. But Chuck's emails lifted us up, not in a sunshine and rainbow way, but in a genuine "I know this is awful, but you are awesome, we'll get through this, I am proud of your work, stay the course" way. He was transparent with the data, and optimistic and inspiring with his words. Because of how he mastered making people feel valued, he was a leader I would follow to the end of the horizon. Much like John at NASA.

Be like Chuck. Flip the script. Practice spotting and flipping negative thoughts so you and your team can stay positive and resilient, By mastering the art of reframing, you see things in a whole new light and achieve even greater success together. Take the negative and make it positive. Don't gloss over the negative, but don't elaborate on it either.

As mentioned Chapter 5, the hallmark of someone with impostor syndrome is how they define their own competence, usually setting unrealistic high standards. Having distorted views of competence and unattainable standards cause you to judge yourself as less intelligent.

In Valerie Young's program "Rethinking Impostor Syndrome™," she proposes a solution that includes reframing, or rethinking the thoughts that got you there. Create a new dialogue that challenges that inner critic that steals self-assurance. Here are some sample scripts that help you to rethink impostor thoughts.

Thought #1: "If it's too hard for me, it must mean I'm not smart enough to do it."
Revised thoughts:
"Facing challenges is how I grow and learn."
"Intelligence is not fixed; it is developed through effort and perseverance."
"Everyone faces challenges."

Thought #2: "If I'm really competent, I shouldn't need to ask for help."
Revised thoughts:
"Seeking help is strength, not weakness, showing my willingness to learn and grow."
"Even the most successful people rely on others for help."
"Certainly there are skilled people who could do this quicker and better than me! I shall find them!"

Thought #3: "If I don't perform perfectly, then I am a failure."
Revised thoughts:
"Perfection is impossible. Progress and effort are way more important."
"Imperfections are part of being human, and they don't define my worth."
"People will forgive me if I make a mistake. Nobody really expects me to be perfect."

Thought #4: "I cannot start the project until I have thoroughly researched every aspect of it."
Revised thoughts:
"Getting started is the first step. Even though I've never done this before, I'm confident I can figure it out."
"Yes, research is essential, but sometimes starting the project will provide valuable insights I wouldn't have gained otherwise. I don't know what I don't know."
"Saying 'I don't know' is not a character flaw, but a tremendous show of admirable humility."

Get Your Best People to Give Their Best Effort

Thought #5: "I must be able to juggle multiple roles simultaneously and perfectly."

Revised thoughts:

"It's okay and healthy to prioritize and focus on one role at a time."

"Nobody can excel at everything."

"I challenge the belief that multitask perfection equals success, and instead, I will celebrate the effort and progress I make in each role."

These are just a few suggestions. But overcoming the stubborn thoughts associated with impostor syndrome is not a once-and-done effort. It takes daily, diligent, and directed effort. Scripts work! Retrain the brain to think better thoughts, make better choices and have better outcomes. When you reset your mindset with a positive inner dialogue, you change the trajectory of your success to go from doubt to dynamo!

24

Teach Someone Something

In his book, *The War of Art*, Steven Pressfield describes *hierarchy* and *territory* orientation. *Hierarchy* orientation involves comparing ourselves to others and determining a pecking order. This natural default stems from our society's chain-of-command structure, where we line up according to criteria like height or skills. As adults, we value people based on adequacy and efficacy, assigning ourselves a place in a hierarchy of worth and dignity.

In contrast, *territory* orientation is independent of others. It's where you function at your best, in your personal space of fulfillment and excellence. This brings deep satisfaction and a sense of purpose. Everyone has a territory of excellence—your dot. It's unique to you, and only you can occupy and control it. You excel in some aspect of art, business, humor, science, cooking, writing, fitness, or politics.

Understanding the difference between hierarchy and territory helps avoid the "compare-and-despair" trap. It's simple, but not easy. You must choose to "ignore your place and embrace your space."

Years ago, I took a class to improve my PowerPoint slides. I volunteered for a critique, and the instructor kindly told me my

Get Your Best People to Give Their Best Effort

slides were not professional. My initial inner impostor syndrome translated this to, "They're awful. What was I thinking? I stink at this."

I decided to challenge my thoughts. I had created the slides myself because I was too proud and cheap to ask for help. It showed. They looked homemade. The instructor pointed out the flaws, offered brilliant suggestions to improve them, and I welcomed his advice. I didn't let his opinion define me because I know my strengths. I'm not a PowerPoint ninja, but I'm a darn good speaker. A stage, a microphone, and an audience—that's my happy place. Accepting that PowerPoint is not my forte, I asked for help with upscaling my slides.

A silly story about slides has a great message. When people can proudly state what specific skills they have, they'll be less likely to be intimidated by other people. They won't be tempted to find a "place in line" or a spot in the pecking order. They'll be able to claim their space, while also appreciating others and their accomplishments. My friend Mike Rayburn is a professional speaker who uses his extraordinary guitar talents in his keynotes. We were talking about how much I love research and he doesn't. He said to me, "When it comes to research, I'm a really great guitar player."

One of the best ways to help your team members fully embrace and appreciate their own abilities and get a grip on runaway impostor syndrome feelings is to have them teach what they know. But here's the caveat. If you ask them to teach it, you'll get pushback, usually in the form of "Not me! I'm not the expert!"

The thought on repeat inside the head of someone who suffers from impostor syndrome is, "They all expect me to be the expert!" It's likely not true. The only one who thinks you need to be the expert is you. The truth is, you don't have to know everything about something. You just have to know something different than those around you. You don't need to be *the* expert. But you can be *an* expert. Even if you know just a little more than those around you, you are *more* expert than others are.

Teach Someone Something

There are four reasons why teaching something to others works wonders.
1. You engage in the act of giving, which always feels good.
2. You confirm to yourself that you do know something well.
3. When you teach something to someone that they already know, they think, "Wow! I know that. I'm smart." You gave them a gift of confidence.
4. When you teach something to someone and they don't know it, they think, "Wow. I didn't know that! That's cool. I feel smart now." You gave them a gift of information.

It's a win-win on every front.

A few years ago, I was the keynote speaker at an information systems association state conference. I had two strikes against me: I wasn't in their industry, and I didn't live in their state. I could have listened to my inner voice saying, "You don't belong here, and they're about to figure that out." Instead, I reminded myself to "teach people something you know."

I gathered my courage and confidence and walked into the conference. I was well-prepared, having spent a lot of time reviewing my material and practicing the talk. Most importantly, I believed in my topic.

My keynote, "Leadership Is NOT Rocket Science," is about leadership and influence. My content wasn't ground-breaking, but I framed it with funny stories, research, and lots of energy.

I even said, "You all know this. I'm not telling you anything new." That's when it hit me. I didn't teach them something new; I reminded them of something they may have forgotten and framed it in a new way. They liked it. I saw it in their body language—they nodded, sat up straighter, and had that "thinking" look in their eyes.

I didn't feel like an impostor. I didn't need to be the smartest person in the room. All I did was show them the value of what they already knew, making it relevant and useful. It was about

Get Your Best People to Give Their Best Effort

them, not me. I was part of their journey, helping them recall useful information that would make their lives better.

You don't know the value of what you know until you share it with someone. Whether or not they already know it doesn't matter. If they don't know it, and you teach them, that's cool. They are now more informed. But if they do know it and you remind them of it, whoa…that's super-cool because now they are more energized, powerful and perhaps even committed to using the information.

Either way, the Impostor can be silenced. So find ways to have your team members teach what they know to others. Reflect on the chapter about dots. Ask your team to identify their dot, and give them the chance to teach about it. Refer back to the chapter on fuel sources, so you can create opportunities for them to get charged up. You will love the results and so will they.

25

Don't Fake it Till You Make It

You've undoubtedly heard the phrase, "Fake it 'till you make it," which means to project the qualities required for success until you get there. If you pretend to have, or fake having, confidence, aptitude or skills, it should eventually lead to success.

But how could faking anything be good for people who struggle with impostor syndrome? Wouldn't that just amplify their impostor feelings? Yes, it does.

What about "acting as if?" Is that the same?

Yes and no.

It comes down to **intention and semantics.** If your intent is to deceive people, or actually fake a skill, or pretend you know something that you don't, that's dishonest, unethical, and not cool. You won't be respected or trusted. And you'll hinder your personal growth because you spend more energy on the façade of competence instead of gaining competence.

On the other hand, "Acting as if" has roots in psychological practices, in substance abuse therapy, where a common perspective was "You can't feel your way into action, but you can act your way into feeling." The concept encourages people to behave in ways that reflect their goals and aspirations, even if they don't initially feel those qualities.

Maybe it's just semantics, but I'd much rather act than fake.

"Acting as if" means *acting* confident regardless of whether you *feel* confident because you want to disarm your doubts by pushing through your doubts. The intent is not on deception, but personal growth. Through regular repeated "acting as if," a person can build a sense of genuine growth and mitigate feelings of impostor syndrome. Whoa. That's good.

Pretending to have a skill (i.e. faking it) is different from hiding a feeling. Doubt is a feeling, and hiding it can be constructive. We hide feelings all the time. We hide sadness; we hide a secret crush on someone; we hide joy over good news that we aren't ready to share yet. Faking it is different from "acting as if."

"Acting as if" can alleviate feelings of fraudulence because it's not borne from a heart of deception. Instead, it's borne from a desire for self-improvement as you search for your real limits and dig deep inside yourself for hidden reservoirs of competence, confidence, and influence. It will be scary like you're leaping off a ledge from your comfort zone into a trench of terror. Do it anyway.

Feelings change last. When you act in a confident way, confidence follows. Of course, the caveat is to act with integrity, not pretending to know what you don't know or do what you're not able to do. Bob Iger, CEO of Disney, says, "There's nothing less confidence-inspiring than a person faking a knowledge they don't possess. True authority and true leadership come from knowing who you are and not pretending to be anything else."

Fake nothing. But act as if you are confident and competent, consistent with the character qualities that shaped you and created your success. People see you as successful and capable. Start acting as if you do too.

Study Guide

As we wrap up this journey of understanding and tackling impostor syndrome within your team, let me give you two more helpful strategies. A great leader recognizes impostor syndrome, but I thought it would be helpful to include a list of definite do's and don'ts that can make a big difference in how your team members see themselves and their abilities. In fact, this could be the most important portion of the book. Consider it your CliffsNotes study guide, your summary of what you don't do, and what you can do for your team members experiencing impostor syndrome.

DON'T do these:
- Assume it's just a woman problem or an under-represented population problem. It's a human problem.
- Punish failure or worship success.
- Ignore it.
- Rush to reassure with platitudes like, "You'll be fine!"
- Make generalized statements like, "You're awesome!" or "I believe in you!" unless you provide evidence.
- Don't discount their feelings with, "You shouldn't feel worried."
- Tease or make light of it.
- Assume they are helpless or unable to change.
- Be dishonest or insincere with your observations.
- Say, "I believe you'll never fail."
- Assume that impostor syndrome can be reasoned away.
- Overwhelm them with what you're learning about impostor syndrome.
- Criticize their past or origins.
- Feel discouraged, blame yourself, or quit if your attempts to help seem futile.
- Get frustrated or impatient when change is slow or absent.
- Nag them about overworking or procrastinating.
- Try to be their therapist.

Get Your Best People to Give Their Best Effort

Rather, DO these:
- Affirm they are not alone.
- Share that you've been learning about it, but only when it's relevant or comes up naturally in conversation.
- Take their doubts seriously.
- Encourage dialogue.
- Ask questions.
- Listen for the emotions underneath their words.
- Watch your own words and body language; make sure you're communicating acceptance and not rejection.
- Tell them your feelings. "I feel sad when I cannot help you."
- Give specific praise after a job well done. Clearly state what they did right, or how it impressed or impacted you and the organization. Verbalize what you admire about them, with examples. "When you made your presentation, I noticed people were riveted to you." "You are known for how you make people feel comfortable." "The way you answered that client's objections was brilliant!"
- Give specific encouragement prior to a big challenge. "Your statistics are always well-researched, so I know you'll be well-prepared for that status meeting." "You are organized and disciplined, so that will serve you well in your new job." "You've handled conflict well in the past. This is not any different."
- Challenge their negative assumptions with questions. "Is it true you'll fail?" "What proof do you have it will happen?" "How likely is it that you'll screw up?" "How will you know when you are prepared enough?" "How often have you fear failing, but ended up succeeding?" "What is the worst that could happen?"
- Challenge the assumption that they will be disliked, disrespected, or discarded if they fail or fall short by pointing out how others have failed (including yourself) and did not experience that same fate. Remind them of

the other positive character qualities that they're known for, because those are the real litmus test of their reputation.
- Challenge them to rethink their definition of competence. Nobody can be perfect. And to think they're the exception to that reflects an ugly pride, not a noble goal.
- Be compassionate if they refer to past experiences or family situations that have led to impostor feelings.
- Suggest therapy if you think it's necessary.
- Hold hope for significant change. It's possible! I know it for a fact!
- Encourage them to keep journals. (I've been keeping a journal for over fifteen years! It's been an extraordinary tool in my personal and professional growth! I've included some journal prompts in Appendix C)
- Hire a coach who specializes in impostor syndrome.

Speaking of coaching, there are some great coaching strategies you can use to support your team. While hiring a professional coach is always a good idea (and I can recommend some fantastic ones), you can still make a huge impact with the right approach and mindset. Appendix B includes a treasure of information to guide and inspire you.

Leading your team through impostor syndrome is about more than just managing; it's about inspiring and empowering them. The journey you're on with your team is one of shared growth and understanding. By creating an environment where everyone feels valued and capable, you can turn self-doubt into a powerful driver of success. Keep encouraging your team, celebrate their wins, and remind them that their unique strengths are what make your team special. As you finish this book, know that your dedication to boosting your team's confidence will lead to a robust, agile, profitable and innovative organization. You will be the champion of getting your best people to give their best effort.

Appendix A

Character Trait Assessment

This character trait assessment is from my self-paced video series "The Fraud-Free Framework." Use this with your team to uncover the often undervalued and overlooked character traits that every person possesses. It can help people push through the times of change and transition that will trigger the impostor syndrome voices.

Traits

Traits differ from skills. Skills can be learned, but character traits are part of your personality. They are affected by your upbringing and biology, and often remain constant through your life. However, because traits reflect your inner convictions, beliefs, and virtues, it's possible that traits change as you age. Maturity, tragedy, spiritual experiences...they all can affect your traits.

This exercise has two tables, one for positive traits and one for negative. Next to each trait listed in the following table, assign a number, from 0 to 4, which reflects the level as you see yourself. A trait can't be less than zero. It can only be on a scale of 0 to 4.

Get Your Best People to Give Their Best Effort

Repeat the exercise, but assign a number (from 0–4) that reflects what you think others would say about you. Ideally, the two numbers should match. But if they don't, circle the higher score. Then think about why the discrepancy exists. Why is your assessment different from how you think others view you? Is it possible that your own assessment is not reliable or accurate? Do you have lower scores for your positive traits compared to what you think others rate you? Is the opposite true of negative traits? Consider talking about this with someone who loves you and knows you well.

Positive Attributes

Trait	HOW I SEE ME	HOW OTHERS SEE ME	Trait	HOW I SEE ME	HOW OTHERS SEE ME
humble			daring		
courageous			trustworthy		
serious			proud		
resourceful			mysterious		
generous			cooperative		
charming			ambitious		
responsible			curious		
demanding			witty		
gentle			determined		
loving			energetic		
loyal			calm		
self-confident			mannerly		
respectful			orderly		
considerate			thoughtful		
spiritual			tolerant		
creative			empathetic		
independent			jovial		
carefree			lively		
studious			reserved		
intelligent			hardworking		
honest			compassionate		

Appendix A: Character Trait Assessment

Negative Attributes

Trait	HOW I SEE ME	HOW OTHERS SEE ME	Trait	HOW I SEE ME	HOW OTHERS SEE ME
arrogant			inconsiderate		
self-centered			disrespectful		
manipulative			aggressive		
dishonest			insecure		
greedy			overbearing		
condescending			gossipy		
pessimistic			insensitive		
jealous			obnoxious		
stubborn			irresponsible		
rude			apathetic		
judgmental			petty		
vindictive			egotistical		
envious			competitive		
impatient			short-tempered		
critical			miserly		
hypocritical			cowardly		
unreliable			defensive		
lazy			sullen		
intolerant			deceptive		
cynical			overcritical		
hostile			domineering		

Gifts and Gaps

Gifts are the skills you possess in abundance. Gaps are the places where you either don't have, don't want, or don't need a skill. Knowing your level of expertise and interest is so helpful. It's not the same as knowing strengths and weaknesses. The key concept of Gifts and Gaps is that there's no negative level. The base level is at zero. Anything above zero is some level of skill, ranging from no skill to mastery level. Using this logic, we all

Get Your Best People to Give Their Best Effort

have gifts, but of varying degrees. Gaps are gifts not yet developed, or the difference between where you are now and where you'd like to be. Grab a notebook and jot down your answers to these questions.

1. List as many of your gifts you can think of.
2. What do others come to you for advice?
3. What's easy for you to do that's not easy for others? (List several!)
4. What's a memorable compliment you received?
5. When's the last time someone said, "Great Job?" What did you do?

Professional Skills and Knowledge

1. What are the specific skills and knowledge that you need to do your job?
2. What formal training/education have you had?
3. What informal training/experiences contribute to your body of knowledge?
4. What are you good at in your job?
5. Did you start the job with that expertise, or did you grow it overtime?
6. What unique knowledge, insights or experience do you have that sets you apart from your coworkers?
7. Do you have DOT envy? Why?
8. What can you say to yourself about this DOT envy that can lessen the intensity of this "compare and despair?"
9. What specific skills/knowledge/information do you have that others need or want?
10. Have you ever shared your expertise with others?
11. How can you create more opportunities to share with or teach others what you know?

Appendix B

Coaching Strategies

Leaders encourage growth, spark innovation and nurture high-potential team members to become extraordinary. In other words, you're a coach. Adopting a coaching mindset can boost your team's performance and morale. Earlier in this book, I recommended you hire a coach, but you may want to take on a coaching approach yourself. You don't need to be a certified coach to make a difference—all you need is the willingness to help your team grow and reach their full potential. This section includes strategies and questions to help you think like a coach who understands impostor syndrome, so you can create a supportive environment where everyone feels valued, confident, and ready to excel.

General Coaching Techniques:

Listen Actively
- Restate what you heard. "I heard you say…"
- State observations: "I saw this, I noticed this."

Get Your Best People to Give Their Best Effort

- Use phrases like, "Tell me more." "That's a great insight." "I see what you mean."

Evoke awareness through questions
- What did it feel like?
- Why do you think you felt that?
- What would you rather feel?
- What will happen if you never change?
- What's the price you're paying for staying the same?

Facilitate Growth
- Tell me more about that.
- Let's back up. Why did that happen?
- Let's pause…what is the story you're telling yourself?
- Have you considered…?
- How does that change things?
- Would you be open to a suggestion?

Explore Options for Thinking Differently
- What would it look like if you…
- What's the worst-case scenario if you were to …?"
- If you could guarantee success, what would you do differently?
- What can you learn in the middle of this challenge?

Goal setting and action plan
- What are your specific goals?
- What are the specific steps to get there?
- What are things you can and cannot control?

Cultivate Trust and Safety:
- Affirm without judgment.
- Don't correct or punish.
- Verbalize your commitment to confidentiality.
- Sit with their vulnerability; don't rush the process.

Challenge Negative Thoughts and Beliefs
- Is it true that…?
- Whose permission/approval are you waiting for?
- Is it feeling or fact?

Coaching Strategies

Specific Coaching Techniques Related to Impostor Syndrome.

Exploring Thoughts and Feelings:
- What specific situations trigger impostor feelings?
- What thoughts typically accompany these feelings?
- How long have you been experiencing these fraud feelings? Are there any patterns or recurring themes?
- Have there been times when you felt confident in your abilities? What was different about those situations?

Challenging Negative Beliefs:
- What evidence supports your accomplishments and skills?
- How would you advise a friend who feels the same way you do about their own accomplishments?
- What are the potential consequences of believing these feelings of inadequacy?
- What would happen if you allowed yourself to accept your achievements without self-doubt?

Goal-Setting and Action-Planning:
- What specific steps can you take to recognize and celebrate your achievements?
- How can you incorporate self-care practices into your routine to help manage feelings of self-doubt?
- What are some realistic goals you can set to build your confidence in areas where you feel uncertain?

Reflection and Progress:
- How can you track your progress in overcoming impostor syndrome? What indicators will you look for?
- What have you learned about yourself through this process of exploring and challenging your impostor feelings?
- What strategies or techniques have been most helpful for you in combating impostor syndrome?

Get Your Best People to Give Their Best Effort

Looking ahead, what strategies will you implement to maintain a healthy self-perception and confidence in your abilities?

Appendix C:

Journal Prompts

Journaling is a powerful tool for dealing with impostor syndrome. By putting thoughts and feelings into words, you can gain clarity, recognize patterns, and challenge negative self-perceptions. This practice allows you to process emotions, track progress, and develop a more balanced and realistic view of your abilities and achievements. The prompts in this appendix are designed to guide you through the "feel-think-do-outcome" process, helping you document and analyze your experiences. Whether you're an individual working to overcome self-doubt or a leader supporting your team, journaling can provide valuable insights and foster a deeper understanding of impostor syndrome, ultimately empowering you to build confidence and resilience.

For Individuals overcoming impostor syndrome

- Describe a moment when you felt like an impostor. What triggered these feelings, and how did you overcome them?

Get Your Best People to Give Their Best Effort

- Describe a recent success. What skills and actions did you use to achieve it?
- List five strengths you bring to your work. How have they contributed to your accomplishments?
- Write about three things you are grateful for about yourself.
- Recall a past achievement that made you proud. How did you feel at that moment?
- Record the compliments you've received this week. How do they make you feel?
- Describe a time when you feared you would fail but succeeded instead. What did you learn from that?
- Write down a negative thought you had about yourself recently. Find evidence that proves it wrong.
- Write about someone who has mentored you. What did they see in you that you couldn't see in yourself?
- Imagine yourself in a future successful scenario. What are you doing, and how do you feel?
- Write about how you learned from a mistake you made. How can you apply this lesson in the future?
- Who is in your support network? How do they help you combat feelings of impostor syndrome?

For leaders leading others with impostor syndrome

- Reflect on a team member's recent success. What strengths did they demonstrate?
- How do you provide constructive feedback that acknowledges strengths and areas for growth?
- How can you encourage your team to recognize and celebrate their own achievements?
- Describe how you mentored someone through a challenging situation. What was the outcome?
- How do you address comparisons among team members to prevent the compare and despair trap?

Journal Prompts

- How can you recognize and reward effort, not just results, in your team?
- What opportunities can you provide for team members to develop their skills?
- How can you foster open communication about feelings of impostor syndrome within your team?
- Write about professional development opportunities that can help team members overcome self-doubt.
- Building a Support Network: How can you help your team build a network of support both within and outside the workplace?
- Reflect on how you can model vulnerability and confidence to your team.
- How can you encourage your team members to reflect on their growth and achievements?
- How do you address failure within the team in a way that promotes learning and growth?
- Share a story of overcoming self-doubt in your own career. How can this help your team?
- What small, manageable challenges can you provide to your team to help them build self-assurance?

About the Author

Maureen Zappala, a New York City native, is an award winning keynote speaker, and author. She has a BS in Mechanical Engineering from the University of Notre Dame and spent 13 years conducting jet propulsion research at the NASA Lewis Research Center (now the NASA Glenn Research Center) in Cleveland, Ohio. She became the youngest and first female manager of the Propulsion Systems Laboratory at NASA.

In 2009 and 2020, she was a top finalist of 30,000+ contestants in the World Champion of Public Speaking contest. In 2024, she became one of only 95 speakers worldwide to earn the Accredited Speaker designation, the top honor for professional speakers in Toastmasters International

She's the founder of High Altitude Strategies, where she speaks to leaders and top performers in corporations and associations on the topic of Impostor Syndrome.

She's the author of "Great Speakers are Not Born, They're Built," "Pushing Your Envelope", and co-author (with Jack Park) of "Buckeye Reflections: Legendary Moments from Ohio State Football." She's a professional member of the National Speakers Association (NSA) and is the 2017-18 President of the NSA-Ohio chapter. She's a fitness fan, avid reader, and enthusiastically average beginner ballroom dancer. In 2019, after 36 years in Cleveland, she relocated to Las Vegas, Nevada. She still hasn't found her winter coat, and that's just fine with her.

Acknowledgments

Former Lockheed Martin CEO, Norm Augustine, in his 1983 hilarious, irreverent and spot-on management book, "Augustine's Laws" writes: "Any task can be complete in only one-third more time than is currently estimated." (Law Number XXIII)

I proved it.

This book started as an idea years ago, but I dragged my feet. When I finally was inspired to get serious about writing it, I didn't think it would take too long. After all, I had piles of content from my blogs, newsletters, research and conversations with clients and audiences. This is my 5th book, and I thought I knew what to expect. I figured it would take eight weeks to get the book done.

It was almost nine months. What a journey!

I often say, "I enjoy the journey because others join the journey." I'm grateful for the people who supported me in this adventure. Time for the thank you's.

To my business coach, Ford Saeks, the real influence and impetus for me to write this book. Thank you for the nudge, the feedback and guidance over these past months. I'm so incredibly grateful for your brilliance and friendship.

Get Your Best People to Give Their Best Effort

To my two mastermind groups and my weekly writing group who cheered me on when I first mentioned the book, and then cheered me on as I slogged through the writing and curating of my content. Even when I was frustrated I wasn't make progress as fast as I wanted, you all supported me. Your enthusiasm was especially touching. You each deserve a shout-out, along with my sincerest respect and deepest appreciation: Darren LaCroix, Ed Tate, Marilyn Sherman, Jennifer Lier, Mark Kamp, Jeff Civillico, Mike Rayburn, Katrina Burrus, Paula Houlihan, Amanda Mae Gray, Stephanie McHugh, Linda Marie Miller, Guy Burns, and Tim Gard.

Thanks to my peers in the National Speakers Association, especially my Las Vegas Chapter. You exhibited unmatched professionalism, diligences, growth mindset, and generosity. I learned from the best of the best in the business world.

Thanks to my precious Toastmaster friends. The organization changed my life, in large part because of the extraordinary people in it. You're my tribe, and I'll forever be grateful that our lives intersect.

Thank you to Valerie Young and Carolyn Herfurth, co-founders of the Impostor Syndrome Institute. The world knows you're smart. But I know you're also funny, kind, enthusiastic, supportive and visionary. It's been a joy to be in your orbit as an inaugural Licensed Associate. I appreciate you both so much.

Thanks to all of my friends for being as excited about this project as I was, and then being excited about it when I wasn't. When I got tired of yet one more read-through of the content, your encouragement kept me going. Every time you asked "How's the book coming?" I was so reenergized all over again.

Thanks to my daughter, Gina, whose extraordinary graphic design talent was the genius behind the cover design. I am SO proud of you! I loved watching you work on this project to bring my vision to reality. I couldn't have asked for a more wonderful partner for this!

Thank you to all my clients and audience members who were my inspiration for getting the book done. I am honored to have rubbed shoulders with so many remarkable people, to give you

Acknowledgments

hope in the middle of your impostor syndrome experience, and hear about how you're defeating the self-doubt demons. Your stories and feedback have been my joy!

Thank you to my immediate family: my sister Pat and her husband George, my brother Kevin and his wife Adeline, my twin brother Sean and my son Ross. While we don't live close to each other, we're never far from each other. I loved your enthusiasm and curiosity about this project. Even if you only pretended to be interested in it, it meant the world to me.

But most importantly, thank you God. All my work is empowered by You, inspired by You, and all for Your glory. I'm Your eternally grateful servant, blessed beyond measure by Your goodness.

And while this has nothing to do with acknowledgments, but everything to do with leadership, I close with another quote from the book, Augustines' Laws: "If the Earth could be made to rotate twice as fast, managers would get twice as much done. If the Earth could be made to rotate twenty times as fast, all the managers would fly off and everyone else would get twice as much done." (Law Number XXXVII)

__Lead well, my friends!__

Other Resources by Maureen Zappala

Keynotes and Workshops

Confidence is NOT Rocket Science!

This program will explore how to recognize impostor syndrome, and recalibrate your thinking so you can begin believing that you really are as smart as everyone thinks you are. You'll move from self-doubt to self-assurance as you match your confidence to your competence and unleash your influence. You won't have to feel like a fraud anymore. Instead, you'll feel great about being great!

Leadership is NOT Rocket Science

The single most significant obstacle to your team's greatest potential is impostor syndrome! As a leader, you'll learn how to recognize it in them, and lead them through it. If you want to build a robust, agile, profitable and innovative team, this program is for you!

Other Resources by Maureen Zappala

Books & Videos

**Pushing Your Envelope:
How Smart People Defeat Self-Doubt
and Live With Bold Enthusiasm**
Learn to recognize and defeat the self-doubt of impostor syndrome. Match your confidence to your competence and unleash your influence.

The Fraud-Free Framework

A self-paced video series that dives deeper into the strategies for overcoming impostor syndrome. A perfect follow-on program for keynote audiences.

**Great Speakers are Not Born. They're Built:
How to Construct Clear, Credible and
Compelling Communications.**

Learn a simple process to put you on the path to becoming an amazing presenter...no matter what kind of presentations you make.

**Buckeye Reflections: Legendary
Moments from Ohio State Football**

Enjoy thus unique compilation of funs facts and beautiful photographs that tell the best stories behind the Buckeye stats

Want your leadership team to shine? Get them this book!

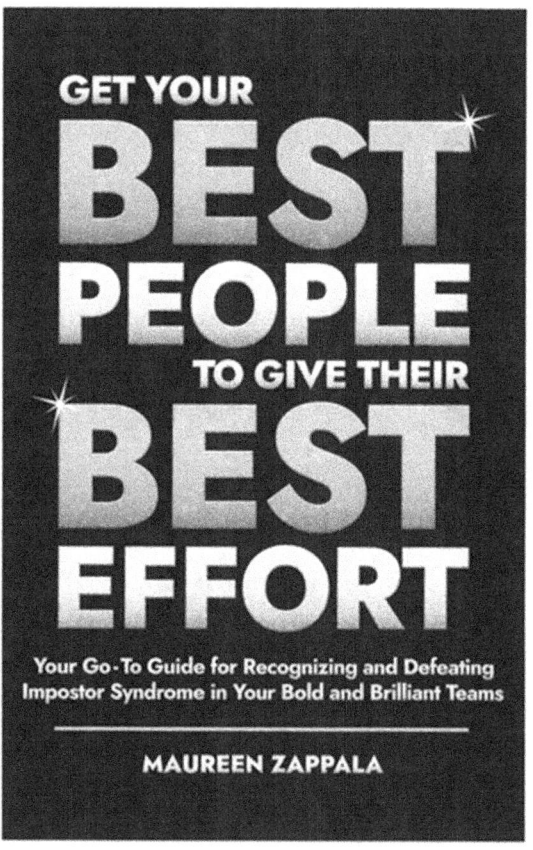

Bulk discounts available.
For more information, email support@maureenz.com
or call 330-441-0722